Volume **11**
of fifteen volumes

LOOK AND LEARN

CHILDCRAFT

The How and Why Library

FIELD ENTERPRISES EDUCATIONAL CORPORATION

Chicago   London   Rome   Sydney   Toronto

Acknowledgments

The publishers of CHILDCRAFT—THE HOW AND WHY
LIBRARY gratefully acknowledge the courtesy of
the following publishers, agencies, and corporations. Full illustration acknowledgments for this
volume appear on pages 314 and 315.

CPN Inc.: photography, page 143, courtesy *Bride's Magazine,* copyright by CPN Inc.
The Frick Collection, New York: *Self-Portrait,* 1658, by
Rembrandt van Rijn, page 107, copyright by The Frick
Collection, New York.
National Periodical Publications, Inc.: illustration, page
155, copyright by National Periodical Publications, Inc.,
1966.
Time Inc.: photography, pages 308–309, by Ralph Crane,
courtesy *Life* Magazine, copyright by Time Inc.
Wrather Corporation: Lone Ranger photo, page 155, re-
produced by permission, copyright 1966 by Wrather Corporation.

CONTENTS

VOLUME 11 *Look and Learn*

LOOK AND LEARN

Look around you.
Look at people's faces
and learn how they feel
or what they're thinking about.
Look at models
and learn about things
that are too big or too small to see.
Look at clothes
and learn something about the people
who are wearing them.
Look at special marks and symbols
and learn what they stand for
and how they're used.
Look at pictures
and learn how people lived and looked
a long time ago.

Keep your eyes open,
because you're surrounded
by people and pictures,
colors and clothes,
shapes and marks,
materials and more things
that you can look at and learn from,
without even reading or hearing a word.

Keep your eyes open—look and learn.

COLORS CAN "TALK"

Can color mean *hot* or *cold*—
without any words?
Can color mean *I love you*—
without any words?
Or can it mean *I'm the king*—
without any words?

In the next few pages
you'll find the answers to these questions
and you'll find much more.
You'll find that color may mean
more than you think it does.

The Lark by Hans Hofmann

Colors That Sing

The artist who painted this picture
called it "The Lark."
Do you suppose the beautiful colors
in the picture
stand for the song of the lark
on a bright summer morning?

Red Hot, and Blue with Cold

People say that red and yellow and orange are "warm" colors,
and that blue and green are "cool" colors.
But if you touch a red wool sweater,
it doesn't feel warmer than a blue wool sweater.
And if you touch a green leaf,
it doesn't feel cooler than a yellow leaf.
Then why *do* people call
certain colors "cool" and other colors "warm"?

Think of some warm things.
Faces turn red when they're warm.
The hot sun glows yellow to orange.
In warm summer weather, strawberries and tomatoes ripen to red.
These may be some of the reasons why we say
red and yellow and orange are warm colors.

Now, why do we say blue and green are cool colors—
    because cold oceans are blue and green?
    because people cool off in the shade of green trees?
    because lips turn blue when they're cold?
Many cold things are blue and green.

There's another reason
we talk about "cool" colors and "warm" colors.
Scientists have measured the temperature of colors
with a special instrument called a thermopile
and have found that reds and oranges
are warmer than blues and greens.

You can't feel the difference,
but "warm" colors really are warmer than "cool" colors.

Hit the Golden Bull's-eye

In the sport of archery,
archers use bows to shoot arrows at targets.
Each colored circle on the target
means a different number of points.
The golden bull's-eye in the center of the target
means *9 points.*
The white circle at the target's outer edge
means only *1 point.*
Each archer shoots a certain number of arrows at the target.
Then the archers collect the arrows.
How do the archers know which arrows are theirs?
That's easy.
Each archer knows the colors
painted on the shafts on his arrows.

Colors also mean players and points in other games such as
chess, checkers, croquet, tiddlywinks, marbles,
card games, billiards, and pickup sticks.

A White Rose or a Red?

Once upon a time, you had to be careful
which flowers you chose to send to someone,
because each kind and color of flower had a special meaning.
A white rose meant *You are charming and good.*
A yellow rose meant *I am jealous.*
A red rose meant *I love you.*
And the colors of carnations, jasmine, lilies, and violets
had special meaning, too.
The pictures on the next page show you what those meanings were.

Even today, a man may send red roses to a woman
to tell her that he loves her.
But we have forgotten most of the special meanings
of other flowers and their colors.
Now, sending flowers to people
simply means we're thinking of them.

A pink carnation on Mother's Day means *mother*.

A white carnation meant *a good luck gift* to a woman.

A red carnation meant *admiration*.

A white jasmine meant *cheerfulness*.

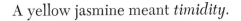

A yellow jasmine meant *timidity*.

A white lily meant *sincerity* and, also, *motherhood*.

A purple violet meant *modesty*.

An orange lily meant *hatred*.

13

Red Tape
Isn't Always Red

Long ago in England,
clerks in law courts and in government offices
used to tie bundles of official papers with red tape.
At that time, "red tape" really meant *red tape*.
Today, when we speak of red tape,
we usually mean something that isn't red and isn't tape.

Today, when we say "red tape"
we may mean the people you have to see
and the official papers you must fill out—
   when you buy a house,
    or borrow money from a bank,
    or apply for a new job.

Over the years,
red tape has come to mean
all the trouble people must go to
when they do business with big organizations.

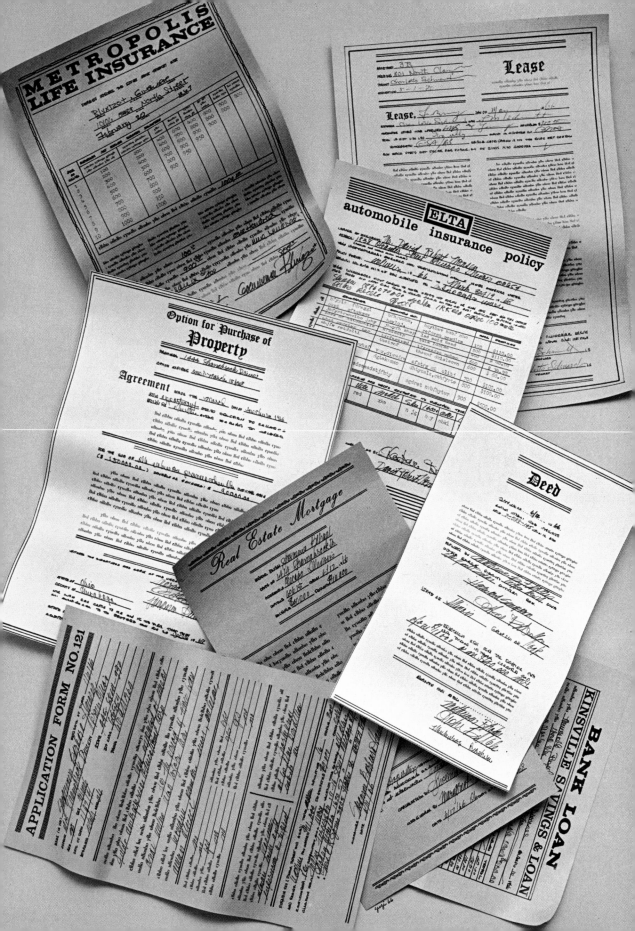

Pay Attention—Red Light

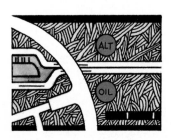

A red light on a car dashboard
warns you when an emergency brake is on,
or when the car needs oil.

On expressways, red lights can mean
that a lane or a tollbooth is closed.

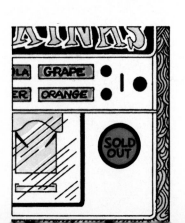

A milk or soda pop machine may have a red light
that warns you when the machine is empty.

On The Air

Radio and television studios have red lights above their doors
that warn people not to barge in while a show is on the air.

EXIT

Sometimes red lights mean, "This way out!"
They do when they're the red lights over emergency exits
in schools, theaters, and other buildings.

And, of course, a red traffic light
is a warning that means "Stop here!"

Although red lights mean different things,
ALL red lights mean "Pay attention—this is important!"

17

Colors for Kings

Imagine being arrested and thrown into jail
for wearing a certain color!
It could have happened back in the days
when kings and emperors ruled.
In ancient Rome, only members of the emperor's family
could wear purple or gold clothes.
In China, only the emperor could wear yellow.
And in France, once upon a time,
only a princess could wear a scarlet dress.
When a person wore clothes in these 'royal' colors,
it was like wearing a sign saying
   "I am the king," or
   "I am the emperor," or
   "I am the princess."
Wearing a special color was much easier than wearing a sign.

One of these men
is the Roman Emperor Justinian I.
Can you identify him
by the color of his clothes?

The Master of Moulins painted this
Portrait of Suzanne of Bourbon,
a French princess of long ago. ▶

Flags of many nations fly outside the United Nations Headquarters, New York.

Red for Courage

You can find the color red
in more than eighty of the one hundred and seventeen flags
of the members of the United Nations.
In many of these flags, red means courage.

Red means courage in the Austrian flag
which has two red bands
separated by a white band.
Austrians say that long ago,
during a battle,
an Austrian duke took off his white tunic
and used it as a flag to lead his soldiers.
The white tunic was stained with red blood
except where the duke's belt had been.

One way soldiers show their courage is by their willingness
to shed their blood for their country.
Blood is red.
Perhaps that is why red has come to mean courage
to the people of so many countries.

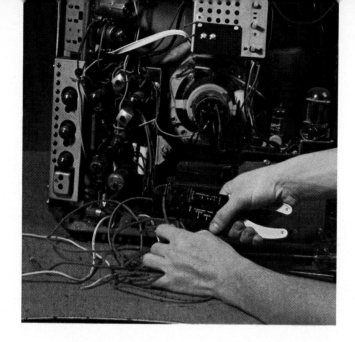

Color Codes

If you could look inside a television set,
or look inside the walls of where you live,
you'd find a network of electric wires.
The network doesn't puzzle an electrician
because the wires are color coded,
and he knows what each color means.
The different colors tell him
where each wire should be connected.

Color coding helps not only electricians—
but many other people, as well.
Salesgirls use color-coded saleschecks.
They may give a pink copy to you
and keep a white one for the store.

Book publishers sometimes color code sections of a book.
They may color the index blue
or green or some other color.

Mapmakers may use color codes.
They may use a different color for each state or country.

Color coding helps many people in business because
a color can mean whatever they want it to mean.

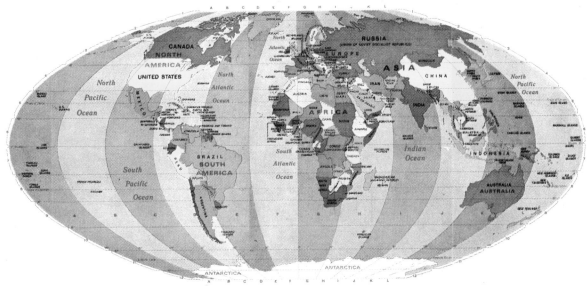

Red Carpet
Treatment

If you went to visit a friend
and found a red carpet rolled out
from the front door to the sidewalk,
what would it mean?
It would mean that your friend
thought you were a very important person.
Long ago, there were no paved sidewalks.
Red carpets were rolled over the mud,
for kings and queens to walk on.
The red carpet kept their long robes
from dragging in the mud.

Today, a red carpet is rolled out on a sidewalk
to honor someone—
perhaps a king, a queen, or a president.

Sometimes red carpets are rolled out
    for brides and grooms,
        for movie stars when their movies are first shown,
        and for astronauts when they return from space.

Why does the carpet have to be red?
That, no one knows.

Astronauts Edward H. White II (left) and James A. McDivitt walk down
the red carpet aboard the aircraft carrier, U.S.S. **Wasp,**
after splashdown in the **Gemini 4** spacecraft on June 7, 1965. ▶

Black Cookies
and Blue Lemonade

Once upon a time there was a boy who loved bread and butter —especially fresh, warm bread spread with creamy golden butter. One morning, he asked his mother to give him a slice of bread and butter. His mother did as he asked.

"This isn't butter," the boy said, "butter is yellow. This is white."

"No, all butter isn't yellow," his mother explained. "This butter is called *winter butter* because it's as white as snow. We've never had this kind of butter before, so you're not used to it. You're used to yellow butter."

All food must have color to look good enough to eat,
but it must be the right color.
You wouldn't want to eat a green orange.
You'd think the green color meant the orange wasn't ripe.
Oranges are supposed to be orange-colored.
But some green oranges *are* ripe.
When growers pick ripe, green oranges, they color them orange.
People expect orange oranges.
The color orange means a ripe, sweet, juicy piece of fruit.

And why don't bakers color cookies black?
Because most people wouldn't eat black cookies:
black doesn't mean cookies (unless they're burned to a crisp).
Why not color lemonade blue?
Because most people wouldn't drink it:
blue doesn't mean lemonade.
Yellow means lemonade and so does pink.

Why do certain colors mean certain foods?
Just because we expect them to.

When Color Means Who's Who

If all football players wore uniforms of the same color,
how would the players and fans tell which team was which?
To avoid such a mix-up, the players on one team
wear uniforms of one color,
and the players on the other team
wear uniforms of another color.
Color tells everyone who's who.

Color also helps people in their work.
The men who work on the flight deck of an aircraft carrier
wear shirts and caps of colors that tell what their jobs are.
    One color means catapult crew;
    a second color means recovery crew;
    a third color means medical corps, and so on.

Construction workers sometimes wear different-colored hats
so the foreman can tell what each man is supposed to be doing.
    A red hat can mean an ironworker.
    A blue hat can mean a laborer.
    A yellow hat can mean an electrician.

Color can be like a label, telling people who's who.

The Chicago Bears are wearing blue shirts with white numbers.
The San Francisco 49ers are wearing white shirts with red numbers. ▶

Joseph's Coat
of Many Colors

In the Bible story of Joseph and his brothers,
Joseph's brothers became jealous when their father, Jacob,
gave Joseph a coat of many colors.
(You can read this story in the Book of Genesis, Chapter 37.)
The brothers were jealous because the coat cost a lot of money
and because none of them had a coat like it.
The coat was a sign that Joseph was his father's favorite son.
Today a coat of many colors doesn't mean anything special.
But in Joseph's time, it meant a lot.

NOTHING
CAN MEAN SOMETHING

Everything and everyone takes up space.
We see space around things, space inside things,
and spaces that go through things.
Sometimes people use space to mean something—
without the use of words.
It's almost as if they make "nothing" mean something.

The next pages will tell you what many niches, notches,
holes, and wide open spaces can tell people.

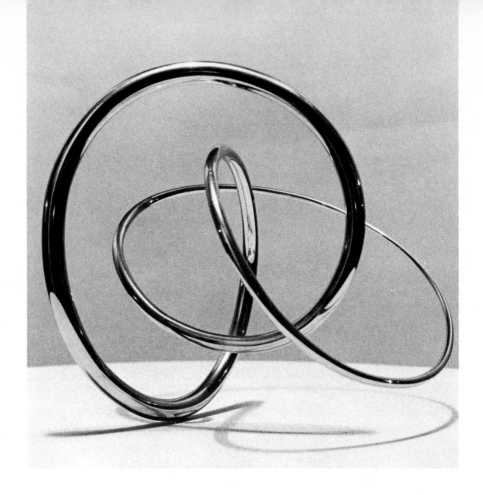

Changing the Shape of Space

Before the sculptor shaped this piece of steel,
it was probably just a long, skinny rod
with lots of space around it.
But now the space turns and curls
around the twisted rod.
By shaping the rod,
the sculptor has shaped the space it stands in.

Different views of the sculpture
Construction, No. 35
by José de Rivera

Read a Punch

Holes punched in a card may mean nothing to you.
But those punched holes can be part of a code
that stands for questions
that a particular kind of computer can answer.

Let's suppose that the holes on one card
stand for this question:
"Which professional baseball player
hit the most home runs in 1961?"

Before the computer can answer that question,
a man called a programmer has to put many answers
about baseball into the computer's memory.

Once the computer has the answers in its memory,
you can feed your punched card into the computer,
and it will "read" the holes.
If your question is one that the computer has an answer to,
you'll get the answer you want:
"Roger Maris"

Keeping Track

The old woman who lived in a shoe
and had so many children
she didn't know what to do
finally found an answer.

She got fourteen hooks
for her fourteen children's coats
and fourteen shelves for
her fourteen children's shoes.

Each night she checked the hooks and the shelves
to see if any coats or shoes were missing.
If she found an empty hook
or an empty shoe shelf,
that meant that one of her children wasn't home.
The empty hook or space on a shoe shelf
told her which child to look for.

Today, empty hooks and spaces on shelves
in a classroom often help a teacher
keep track of her pupils and their things.

An empty hook or a space on a shelf
can mean a lot without words being spoken.

Space on a Page

All that white space
around the words on the opposite page isn't a mistake.
The designer of the page did it on purpose.
Here's why:
When you see a page, you expect to see something on it—
many words, or a picture of some kind.
When you see space instead,
you can't help looking for something in the space.
The space has attracted your attention.
It is as if the surprising space had said to you, "Look!"

And "Look" is what white space means
in many advertisements on billboards,
in magazines, and even on television screens.

Sometimes a person starts to think about buying something
when he sees a picture of it surrounded by a lot of white space
that catches his attention.

Read CHILDCRAFT

To Play, To Build, or To Plant?

What does a vacant lot mean?

Almost everyone will agree that it's an open space,
but people don't agree when you ask
what this open space means.

To a child it can mean a place to play football in autumn,
a place to fly a kite in spring, or
a place to ice skate in winter.
To a grown-up it can mean a place for a building,
a parking lot, a playground, a park,
a vegetable garden,
a hot dog stand,
a service station,
or just about anything.
What does a vacant lot mean?
Well, that depends on you.

41

A Hole To Crawl Into

I can be anyone I want to be
and do anything I care to do
as I hide in my make-believe cave.
    I'm Alice falling down the rabbit hole.
    I'm a spaceman in a crater on the moon.
    I'm the genie in Aladdin's Lamp.
    I'm a secret agent tracking down a spy.
    I'm Jonah sitting in the stomach of a whale.
    I'm in a submarine at the bottom of the ocean.

This make-believe cave can mean anything
I want it to mean.

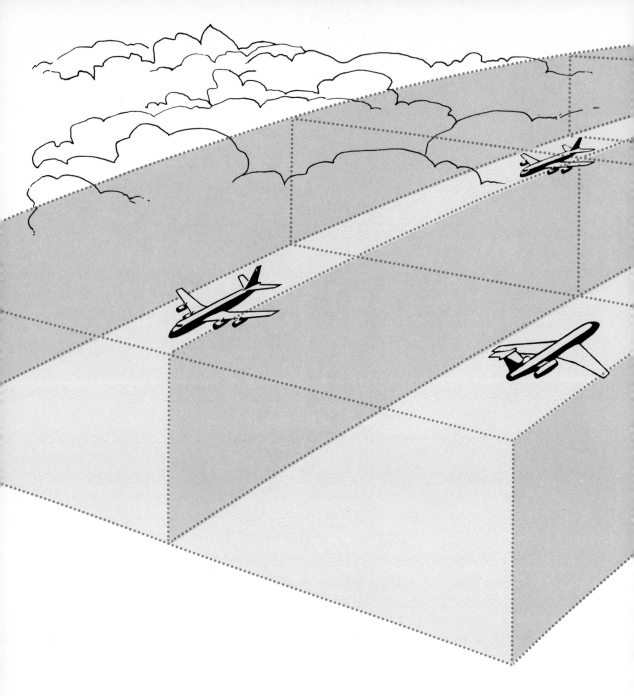

Moving Box of Space

Did you know that when an airplane flies,
it flies inside a box?
It's not a wooden box or a metal box.
In fact, you can't even see this box.
It's a box of space.

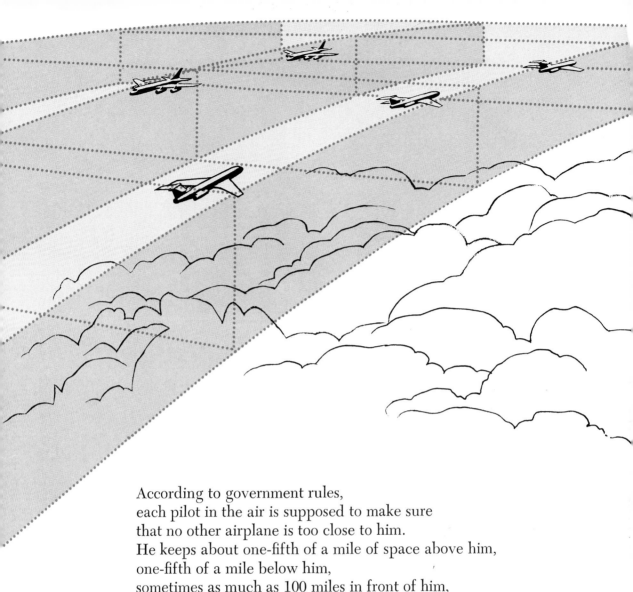

According to government rules,
each pilot in the air is supposed to make sure
that no other airplane is too close to him.
He keeps about one-fifth of a mile of space above him,
one-fifth of a mile below him,
sometimes as much as 100 miles in front of him,
and 100 miles in back of him.

As the picture shows, all that space surrounding an airplane
makes a kind of invisible box around it—
a box of space that travels right along with the airplane.

To make sure his airplane is in the box,
the pilot constantly checks his radar,
or he keeps calling on the radio
to air traffic control centers on the ground.

What does that invisible moving box of space mean? SAFETY.
As long as that much space is around an airplane,
it can't crash into another airplane.

45

The Space Around

It's a vase.
No, it's a face.
No, it's two faces.
No, it's a vase.

The picture you see could be either a vase or two faces,
depending upon how you look at it.

If you think of the black as space, you will see a vase.
But if you think of the white as space, you will see two faces.
You might say it's like looking in reverse.

Some sculptors have a reverse way of looking at things, too.
They try to picture the space around a statue they are making.
The spaces around a statue help to form
the figure the sculptor wants.

You, too, can look at things in the same way those sculptors do.

Look at a tree.
Then look at the space around it
and the spaces between the branches.

Or look at the shapes of the spaces between houses.
Try it with anything you want—even a piece of sculpture.

Goats Butting, a bronze
sculpture by Anna V. Hyatt
Huntington

IFALLNOWHERE

IF ALL NOW HERE

I FALL NOWHERE

Spaces Make Sense

The letters on top of the opposite page
look like a nonsense word—
a word that doesn't mean anything.
But if you put spaces between certain letters,
the "word" can become part of a sentence:

    IF ALL NOW HERE

Or, if you put the spaces in other places,
the "word" can become a complete sentence:

    I FALL NOWHERE

Those spaces help you know what the letters mean—
they show you where one word ends and another begins.

Long ago, people used to write with no spaces between words.
    Wordspushedtogetherlikethislookstrangetous.
We are used to seeing the spaces between words.

Spaces between words mean less confusion and easier reading.

Fill It Up or Leave It Alone

To some people, an empty shelf means
a space to use by filling it with as many
things as it will hold.

To other people, an empty shelf means
a space to use by leaving it open,
except for one thing worth special attention.

Both ways of using space are important.
Sometimes you have to fill it.
Sometimes you want to leave it open.

It takes careful planning of space to keep
a small trailer from looking filled-up.

50

You can leave space open in a large room
and make the room seem even larger than it is.

Who's Afraid of a Bank?

Once, people were a little afraid to go into banks.
Some say one reason was that banks were usually
dark buildings with thick walls
and dark columns in front.
Their inside windows
were covered with iron bars like those of a jail.
Some people were even afraid to put their money there.

Today, many new banks have more space
and see-through places that mean
"you're welcome here—and so is your money."

Hardly anyone is afraid of banks anymore.

The Shape of a Space

The shape of this jello has the same shape as the space inside the jello mold.

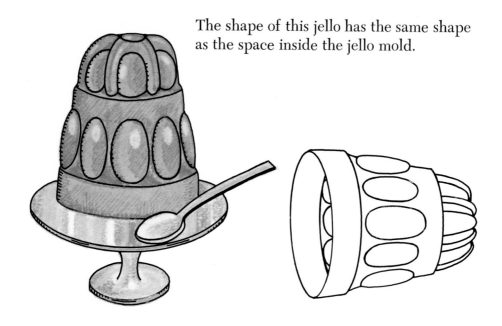

Cherry ice suckers have the shape of the spaces inside the ice cube tray.

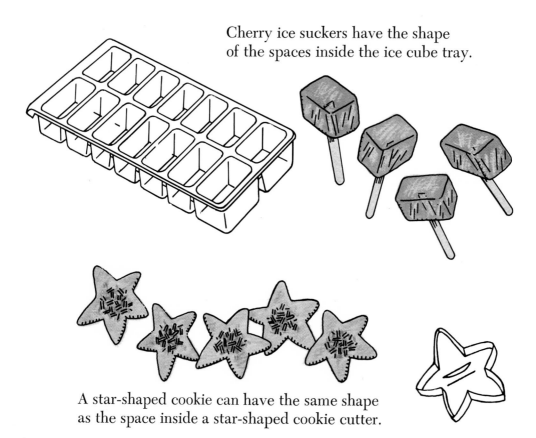

A star-shaped cookie can have the same shape as the space inside a star-shaped cookie cutter.

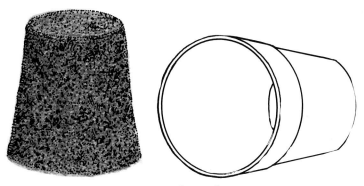

The shape of wet soil can have
the shape of the space inside a flowerpot.

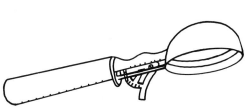

A dip of ice cream can show you the shape
of the space inside an ice cream scoop.

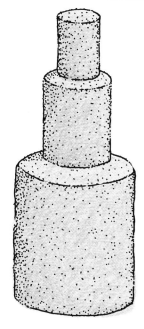

A sand castle can have the shape of space
inside three tin cans.

Many times you can tell what the shape of the space is
inside a container, just by looking at the shape
of the stuff that has been dumped out of it.

Many machines have spaces to put coins in.

Spaces That Decide for You

Pay telephones have a slot to fit the smallest coin—
and that means a dime.
The next largest slot is meant for nickels.
And the largest slot is meant for quarters.

Half dollars won't work because
they are too big to fit into the slots.
Pennies will fit into the larger slots
but the telephone company won't let you use pennies
to make a phone call.

So if you use a pay telephone to call a far away city,
you must have the coins that will fit into slots.

SHAPES FROM A TO Z

Letters from A to Z are really a code—
but not a secret code.
They make the most *un*-secret code there is.
The whole idea of the letter code
is that everyone should know it.
Then when one person puts letters together
in a certain way to express an idea,
anyone else in the world can know
what that person's idea was,
just by knowing the code.

Just think! All the ideas that human beings have,
or ever had, can be saved and used again and again—
all because of a code of different-shaped scratches
that we call letters.

The next few pages will answer questions
you may never have thought to ask
and tell you about the shapes and forms
of letters—and numerals!

Detail of Trajan's Column in Trajan's Forum, Rome, Italy

Letters in Stone

The Roman capital letters on the stone tablet
on the pedestal of the Trajan column
were carved in Rome nearly 2,000 years ago.

Many people say that these letters
are the most beautiful letters ever designed.

Today, many art students still practice
drawing the Roman capital letters
that the Romans carved in stone long ago.

Trajan's Column

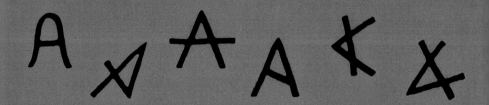

Where Our Alphabet Comes From

The English alphabet we know came from the Roman alphabet.
The Roman alphabet came mostly from the Greek alphabet.
And the Greek alphabet came from marks
that people from many other lands made.
Many people had ways to write down
ideas that they wanted to save.

In any alphabet, each letter
is supposed to stand for a certain sound.
But people make sounds in slightly different ways,
so sometimes one letter may stand for several sounds.
For instance, you can say the sound of the letter A
in about four different ways—the ways you would say it
if you spoke the words, "hay," "hat," "harm," and "hall."

That's one reason why spelling is sometimes hard.
Some experts tell us that people who speak English
make about 42 different sounds.
But we have only 26 letters to stand for those sounds.

So really our alphabet comes from the sounds people make.
The letters are just shapes that stand for sounds.

An Alphabet Trick

Question: How can you spell an eight-letter word with only one letter and part of another letter?

Answer: Spell the word "alphabet" out loud in Greek—"alpha" is the name of the first letter of the Greek alphabet and "bet" is short for "beta," which is the name of the second letter of the Greek alphabet. That's how we got the word "alphabet"—from the names of the first two letters in the Greek alphabet.

The letters that border these pages show how the shapes of the letters A, B, C, and D have changed.

A Language in Pictures?

Just think! If we had a picture language
instead of an alphabet,
you wouldn't have to worry about learning to spell.
And you wouldn't have to learn to read words.
School would be easy.
All you would have to do to read
would be to look at pictures.

But would it be so easy?
Let's try it.
Without words let's write,
"A man rides a horse."
That's easy; you'd write it like this:

But what if you wanted to write,
"A man named Joe rides a horse"?
You can draw a picture of a man on a horse
but how can you draw a picture of the name "Joe"?
One way is to invent some scratches to mean "Joe"
and write them above the man like this:

Now you don't have just a picture language any more.
You've had to add scratches
that don't look like anything but scratches,
and yet the scratches give you some meaning
that the picture couldn't give you.
The letters we use in our language
are scratches-that-give-meaning, too.
The scratches or marks we use
to stand for the name "Joe" look like this:

JOE

And how would you write,
"Many men ride many horses"?
Would you draw three, four, or five pictures
of men on horses?
And if you drew five pictures, how would you know
that five meant just "five," rather than "many"?
How many is "many"?

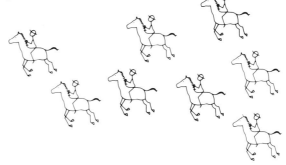

Again you would need some scratches that meant "many."
With letters we have such scratches. They are:

MANY

Maybe it's easier to learn spelling
than to learn picture language, after all.

Which Way Do You Read?

What does plowing a field have to do with the way we read?

Once long ago, after the Greek alphabet was invented,
the Greek people began writing words and sentences.
When the sentences they wrote took up more than one line,
they thought it would be better
to write the second line backwards.
If their sentences had been in English,
they would have read something like this:

COME OVER TO MY HOUSE
YTRAP A GNIVAH M'I ESUACEB
TOMORROW.

To us that seems silly,
but they had a reason that seemed good to them.
When they plowed their fields
they would go first one way and then back.
So why shouldn't they read that way, too?

In time, though, people learned that it was easier to read
sentences if the words went the same way in every line.
That's the way we do it now.

So plowing a field now doesn't have anything to do
with the way we read.
And aren't we glad it doesn't?

From an Ox to an A

Letters are codes for sounds.
A long time ago, long before Jesus was born,
the most important property a person could own was an ox,
because oxen helped plow fields.
The sound that people in Egypt
made when they meant "ox" would be spelled, "aleph"—
something like a way we say "a," plus the sound "lef."
When the Egyptians decided to make an alphabet,
they decided that the first letter would be "aleph."
And when they wrote the letter, they made it look
like the head of an ox, as in this picture.

How did the head of an ox come to look like our "A"?

It took more than 1,500 years
for some people called Semites
to take the eye away
and make it simpler, like this:

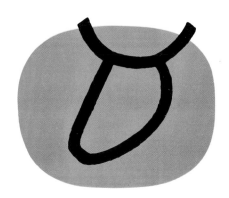

In another 500 years
some people called Phoenicians
made it still simpler
and turned it on its side.

And more than 2,000 years after that,
the Romans finally made the ox head
into the shape we now know as "A."

Many of our letters started with pictures the way "A" did.
But no matter how their shapes have changed,
the letters have always been codes for sounds
that people make when they talk.

Mind Your P's and Q's

When someone says, "Mind your p's and q's,"
it usually means "be careful of what you do or say."
But to a printer, "Mind your p's and q's"
is a warning to watch that he doesn't mix up
the small letter p and the small letter q.

To print letters, a printer uses little metal blocks
with raised letters on one end.
These little letter blocks are called type.
As you can see in the picture,
the raised letters are backwards or in reverse.

If you look at the pieces of type for the letters p and q,
you can see that the p on the type looks like q
and the q looks like p.
But when they are printed, they reverse on the paper
and look like themselves again.
You can see how easy it might be for a printer
to confuse the p and the q.
And if he turned the p upside down,
the shape would look like the letter d.
And if he turned the q upside down,
the shape would look like the letter b.

Just think what a printer could do
to the word used for the sound that a duck makes.
The word might come out *puack, duack,* or *buack* instead of *quack.*

Printers have to mind their p's and q's
or they might not print the word they mean to print.

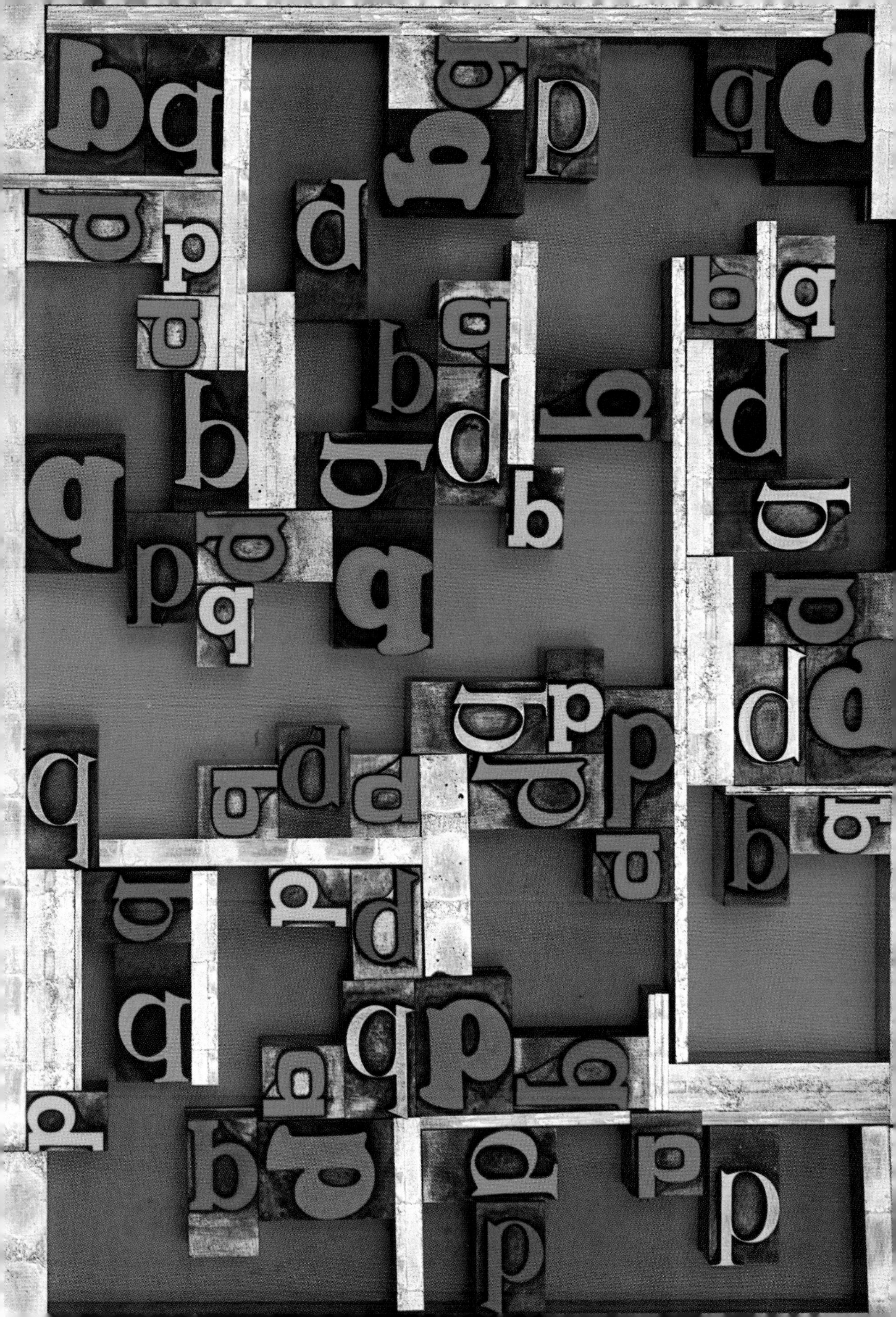

Big Letter, Little Letter

There was a time when all letters
were capital letters and were lettered by hand.
Men called scribes spent ther lives
writing books in capital letters.

One famous English scribe and scholar
by the name of Alcuin studied and studied the letters
and finally found a faster way of copying words onto a page.
When he went to France nearly 1,000 years ago,
he taught other scribes his new way of writing letters.
"Look at the letter B," he might have said to the scribes.

B written this way takes
three strokes

B written this way takes
two strokes

B written this way takes
one stroke

Alcuin worked with all the letters of the alphabet
until he could write each one with a few strokes of the pen.
His letters were rounded and sometimes attached:

abcdef

The small letter alphabet that we use today
comes from the small letters that Alcuin designed long ago.
Having small letters means that we can write more words faster.

This picture of a scribe at work looks as if it
were printed from a design carved into a block of wood,
the way many pictures were made long ago.

The Faces of Letters

To print letters, such as the letters on this page,
a printer uses little metal blocks
with raised letters on one end.
Those blocks are called pieces of type.
And the top of a raised letter
is called the type face.

A printer can give any letter many "faces."
For example, the A's face can look happy, . . .

or serious, . . .

. . . or formal.

The letter A can have more faces than you can think of,
but you can still recognize it as the letter A.

Printers have a choice of hundreds of type faces.
The kind of face a printer chooses for a letter
depends upon what he wants the reader to feel.

Let's see how some different type faces look.

These letters might mean
a pillow fit for a king's crown.

These letters might mean
a pillow as hard as a rock.

THESE LETTERS MIGHT MEAN A LONG SKINNY PILLOW.

These letters might mean
a lacy pillow for a baby.

These letters might
mean fancy little pillows.

THESE LETTERS MIGHT MEAN A BIG
PILLOW FOR A CIRCUS LION TO SIT ON.

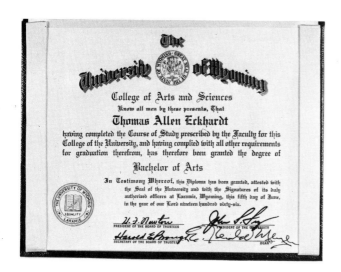

A diploma for a school graduation

A special tribute to a famous person

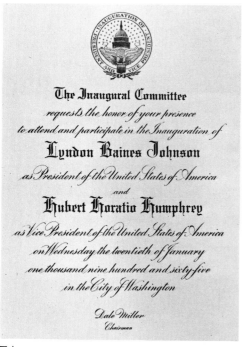

An invitation to an inaugural ball

For Special Occasions

The kind of lettering in the pictures on these pages
isn't like ordinary handwriting
or like any printed letters that you usually see.

Those letters were "dressed up" for special occasions
by handwriting experts called calligraphers.
The word "calligrapher" comes from a Greek word
that means "beautiful writer."

The lines of a calligrapher's letters
swirl and curl into decorative designs.
His letters spell words that say something special.

A special award

uiuficatur. Jtē pal-
ladius pulices fugan-
tur. amurta p̄ pau-
mentum frequenter aspa
sa cum cumio agresti
ul' cum aqua. Vl' cucu
meris agrestis semie
aqua resoluto sepe in
fuso. Explicit. xiiij
tractatus. incipit ij. xv.
tc.ꝗ ue. et te. ꝗ incipiunt ab hc lra. R.
pant ab hc lra. R.
De remedijs Juen
te. ꝗ incipiunt ab hac
lra. R. vj. v'. tractatus.
Contra rauiam :—
ana a
garrii
tatre
ruocata
est. eo
quod aura genitales

palutes strepit et fo-
nos uocis importunis
clamoribus reddit fm
hysiꝰ. libro. xij. Jte
er libro te natura rex.
ranax coitus magis
est te nocte ꝗ te die
in earum coitu magn̄
est mora. multum se-
mis effundunt. ranas
hr mare que alas ha-
tent. et otius pistas fe-
tus nutrie ꝓter ranam.
Jtem auic̄. m .uij. ca-
nonis. uenenū tang-
cognoscitur p abhomi-
nabilem saporem sicut
leporis marini potret.
Sunt rane fluuiales
uintes et marine ru-
bre utreꝗ uenenose.
Garum potu accidit ob

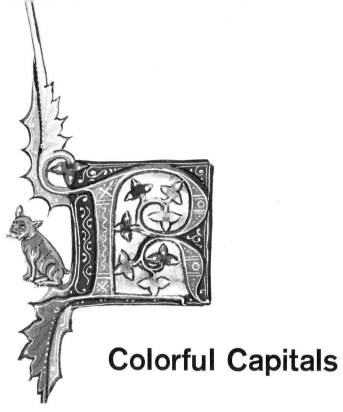

Colorful Capitals

"Color my capital letters with gold," commanded the king.
"Make mine silver," said the queen.
"Brighten mine with many colors," cried the little princess.

Kings and queens who lived hundreds of years ago,
might have ordered books to be decorated
with a certain color.
Books at that time were written and decorated by hand
by men known as scribes.
The picture on the opposite page shows the work of one scribe.
Notice the capital letter.
It is so big and so full of color
that it seems to light up the page.
Maybe that's why decorated letters such as this
were called "illuminations."
The word "illuminate" comes from a Latin word
that means "light up."
And that's what scribes did—they illuminated
or lighted up capital letters with bright colors.

Illuminated books take a long time to write and decorate,
and are so expensive that few people can afford to buy them.
Hardly anyone owns a book that is illuminated any more—
except libraries, museums or rare book stores.

Where Numerals Come From

To say how old I am,
I can write this shape.

To say how many brothers I have,
I can write this shape.

To say how many beetles
I have in my jar,
I can write this shape.
Having these shapes makes it easier for me
to tell people things about me.
Those shapes are called numerals.
A numeral is the shape or mark we write to stand for a number.

Many different stories tell
how our numerals got their shapes.
Here's one story.
If someone wanted to buy one chicken,
he would raise one finger to show how many.
From a lifted finger came the shape of the numeral 1.

Numerals 2 and 3 came from straight lines.
People used to write two lines to mean two things, like this: ══
and three lines to mean three things, like this: ≡
When they wrote the two lines rapidly,
the shape looked like this: ⇁
When they wrote the three lines rapidly,
the shape looked like this: ⧼

Another story tells about a man who needed a numeral
for eight things so he just made up a shape like this.
Maybe the other shapes were invented that way, too.

The shapes of numerals have changed in the past 700 years.
Having numerals means that people can do more than count.
They can figure how deep a well is, how much an elephant weighs,
how many words in a book, how far it is to the moon—
or just about anything they want to figure.

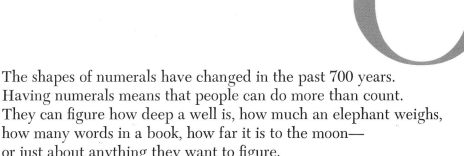

1 2 3 4 5 6 7 8 9 0   Twelfth-century numerals

1 2 3 4 5 6 7 8 9 0   Fourteenth-century numerals

1 2 3 4 5 6 7 8 9 0   Numerals today

The Importance of Nothing

If you want to write a shape to mean *nothing*,
you write the shape "0."
Long ago people agreed that that shape would mean *no* things.
We call the shape "zero."

What may seem strange at first,
is that because a "0" means *no* things, or *nothing*,
you can use it with other numerals to mean *many things*—
if you put the "0" in the right place.

You can write a "0" after a "1", like this—"10"—
to mean *ten*.
   The "0" in "10" means *no* ones,
   and it makes the "1" mean *one* ten.
You can write another "0" after the "10", like this—"100"—
to mean *one hundred*.
   Then the last "0" in "100" means *no* ones,
   it makes the middle "0" mean *no* tens,
   and it makes the "1" mean *one* hundred.
If you keep on writing zeros, the bigger the number will be.
That's one reason the shape that means *nothing* is important.

Hundreds	Tens	Ones
		1
	1	0
1	0	0

HANDS AND FACES

You can say a lot—
without speaking a word—
just with the look on your face.
    You smile, you frown,
    you wince, you scowl.
    You raise an eyebrow.
    You wrinkle your forehead,
and anyone who looks at the expression on your face
knows how you feel, or what you're thinking.

You can also say a lot—
without speaking a word—
just by the motions, or gestures,
you make with your hands
or any other part of your body.

The next few pages will tell you
what different expressions and gestures mean
and how people use expressions and gestures
to mean certain things—
without speaking a word.

A Father's Curse: The Ungrateful Son
by Jean Baptiste Greuze

Good-bye!

The young man waving good-bye is leaving home
with his friend, who is standing in the doorway.
But the young man's family wants him to stay.

Can you tell from the hands and faces
who might be saying or thinking each of these things?

"I warn you, you'll be sorry. Stay home, son!"

"Please, Father, you mustn't get so upset."

"I wonder how Father would act if I left home."

"Please, please, *please* don't go!"

"If you go, who's gonna give me piggy-back rides?"

"Son, look at what you're doing to your father!"

"Sorry, I must go. Good-bye!"

"Tsk, tsk. What a family."

Making Cartoon Faces

Here are some eyes that are—

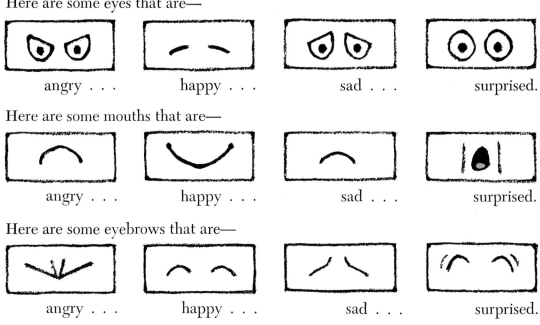

angry . . .   happy . . .   sad . . .   surprised.

Here are some mouths that are—

angry . . .   happy . . .   sad . . .   surprised.

Here are some eyebrows that are—

angry . . .   happy . . .   sad . . .   surprised.

Put them together and what do you have?

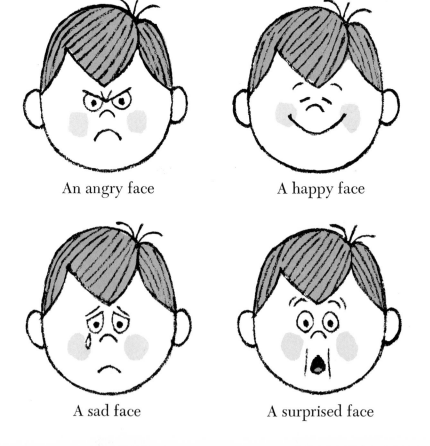

An angry face   A happy face

A sad face   A surprised face

Cartoon artists everywhere draw faces
with the same kinds of eyes, mouths, and lines
to help tell a story or to make you laugh.

You can be a cartoon artist, too.
Draw some face shapes, hair-dos, and ears.
You may even want to draw a dog face or an elephant face.
Then add the eyes, mouths, and lines in the pictures to make
your own furious face, happy face, sad face, and surprised face.

For Safety's Sake

Traffic policemen tell drivers when to stop,
when to go, and when and where to turn.
But drivers can't hear a policeman
because of the noise of engines,
rattling trucks, and honking horns.
That's why traffic policemen use arm gestures
such as these to direct traffic.

This means "Stop."

This means "Go."   This means "Turn left."

This means "Turn right."

But traffic policemen
aren't the only ones who use their arms for "talking."
Drivers and bicycle riders sometimes use arm gestures
that tell things to other drivers and to people crossing streets.

This means "I'm turning left."

This means "I'm stopping."

This means "I'm turning right."

Anyone who uses streets, sidewalks, and highways
should know what these arm signals mean—for safety's sake.

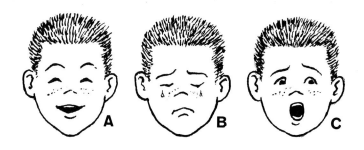

Your Face Can Say Things

Sometimes you can tell what a person's thinking
or how he's feeling—just by the look on his face.

The expressions on the face of the boy
in the pictures at the top of these pages mean different things.
See if you can tell what the boy's thinking.
For answers see pages 312–313.

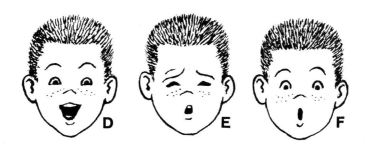

Try this experiment yourself.
Stand in front of a mirror
and make faces—or expressions—
that mean these things:
"I feel sad."
"Boy, am I hungry."
"You wanna fight?"
"May I please, please have another piece of cake?"

Can you think of other things
that you can say with your face?

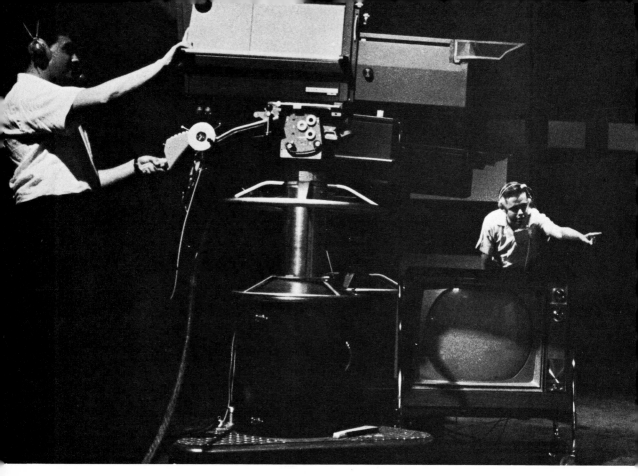

A floor director in a television studio signals
to tell a newscaster he's on the air.

Silent TV Talk

A television director
has to make sure that a TV program
lasts only as long as it's supposed to,
whether it's five minutes of news,
or ninety minutes of drama.

To help him make the program come out on time,
he works with another director, called a floor director.
The floor director works in the studio
behind the cameras,
while the director works in
a glassed-in control room that looks into the studio.

"Slow down. You have plenty of time."

"You're right on time."

The director and the floor director
talk to each other during rehearsals
through special headpieces that they wear.
When the program is on the air,
the floor director gets instructions
from the director in the control room.
Then the floor director tells the actors
what to do by making gestures.

"Hurry up. You're running out of time."

"Stop."

You don't see the floor director
on your television screen
because he works behind the cameras
where he won't be seen.
And he uses gestures so that he won't be heard
by people watching television.

Starting a Fight

Long ago, if you were a knight
and you threw one of your gauntlets to the ground
in front of another knight,
it was like saying, "I challenge you to a duel."
A gauntlet was a heavy leather glove
usually covered with pieces of iron.
The gesture came to be called "throwing down the gauntlet."
If the other knight picked up the gauntlet
that you threw down,
it was his way of saying, "I accept the challenge."

Nowadays, we seem to do just the opposite.
Instead of "throwing down the gauntlet,"
we "put on the gloves" for a fight—
the boxing gloves.

Just for fun, two boys put on boxing gloves
at a Navy Junior Boxing Final at Annapolis, Maryland.

Acting Without Words

Pantomime artist Yass Hakoshima
imitates a puppet whose arm is
held up by a make-believe string.

Could you act out a play
without saying a word?
It seems impossible, but special actors
have been acting out wordless plays
for hundreds of years.
These plays are called pantomimes.

In a pantomime, actors tell a story
with expressions and gestures.
They move their arms, legs, and bodies,
and change the expressions on their faces
to tell the people in the audience
who they are,
what they feel,
and what they are doing.

Sometimes one person acts the parts
of all the characters in a play.
He becomes the hero, the villain,
the heroine, or anyone else in the play.
How do you know when the actor changes
from one character to another?
By the different expressions
and gestures that he uses.

Hakoshima plays the part of a happy fisherman who has finally caught something in his net. But how does he feel when he sees what he has caught?

Talking With Hands and Fingers

Deaf people can "talk" to each other,
even though they can't hear.
They move their hands and fingers
to make signs that tell each other
what they can't hear.

Some signs stand for words.
Some signs stand for letters of the alphabet.
Some signs stand for numbers.
Deaf people usually use a combination
of these signs
when they "talk" to each other.

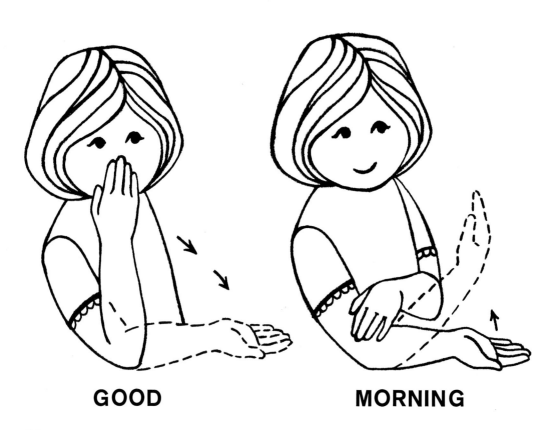

GOOD   **MORNING**

WHY

DO

BIRDS

FLY

SOUTH

? For answer see pages 312–313.

Masks for Actors

If you acted in a play in Greece long ago,
you'd wear a mask.
If you played the part of a sad person,
you'd wear a mask with a sad-looking face.
If you played the part of a happy person
you'd wear a mask with a happy-looking face.
But if you played the part of a happy person
who suddenly got some bad news
you'd quickly change from a happy mask to a sad mask.

The masks of Greek actors were much bigger
than the faces of the actors.
And the expressions on the masks were overdone
so that people sitting in the back row
could see and understand what was happening on stage.

But this was not the only reason
that Greek actors wore masks.
An actor wore masks so that he could change
from one character to another during the play.

This meant that one actor could play a young man and an old man.
Whenever he changed parts,
he just changed masks.

Maybe you've already seen pictures of these masks.
They stand for the plays that you can see in a theater—
including happy, funny ones and plays with sad endings.

Some actors today wear masks like those the Greeks wore long ago.

Sports Signals

A football referee
can "talk" with his arms.
If you see him
do this during a game,
he's telling you
"There's been a delay in the game."

If he does this, he means
"The ball is out of play."

But if he does this, he means
"Someone has made a touchdown
or a field goal."

Officials in other sports also "talk" with their arms.

In basketball,
this gesture means
"No score."

In baseball,
the same gesture means
"He's safe."

But in football
the gesture means
"incomplete forward pass."

These sports signals mean something
to everyone who knows the rules—
officials, players, and sports fans.
But some gestures are secret signals
between the players or coaches of a team.
Only those who are in on the secret
know what the secret signals mean.

A baseball catcher sometimes makes a gesture
that tells the pitcher what kind of pitch to throw.
Or a baseball coach can make a gesture that
tells a runner to keep running or to steal a base.

Players and coaches in many different team sports
use secret signals to tell each other things
that players on the opposite team
aren't supposed to understand.

See What I Mean?

What would you do if you were in a foreign country
and you didn't know how to speak the language?
You might use expressions and gestures
like these to make others understand you.

This could mean you're hungry
and you'd like to find a restaurant.

This could mean you're tired
and you need a place to rest.

This could mean you have a toothache and you want to go to a dentist.

If the person who's trying to understand you makes a face like this,
you know that he sees what you mean.

But if someone makes a face like this, you'd better try other expressions and gestures. As you can see, she doesn't know what you mean.

What Should a Gentleman Do?

A gentleman sometimes tips or takes off his hat
to show respect to someone.

A gentleman takes off his hat
when he stops outdoors to talk to a woman he knows.

He tips his hat when he lets an old lady
sit down in his place on a crowded bus.

A gentleman takes off his hat
when a lady enters the elevator of an apartment house.
But he leaves his hat on
in the elevator of a bank or a store.

A gentleman should always take off his hat
when the national anthem is played in a public place
or when the flag is carried past him on parade.

A gentleman must know
when to remove his hat, when to tip it,
and when to leave it on his head.
And if a gentleman can't remember
when to do what with his hat,
maybe the gentleman shouldn't wear a hat.

The Story of an Artist

One of the world's most famous artists,
Rembrandt van Rijn,
lived in Holland long ago.
We know a lot about Rembrandt
from the many pictures he painted of himself.
Pictures that an artist paints of himself
are called self-portraits.

You can see more than a hundred self-portraits of Rembrandt.
He painted some portraits when he was young
and some when he was old,
some when he was happy, and some when he was sad.
And they all help to tell us the story of his life.

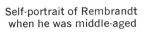
Self-portrait of Rembrandt
as a young man

Self-portrait of Rembrandt
when he was middle-aged

Self-portrait of Rembrandt
as an old man

Shaking Hands

Long ago, men shook hands
as a way of saying, "You can trust me."

One man held out his hand to another
to show that he wasn't ready to pull out his sword.
If the other man held out his hand, too, they shook hands.
Each saw that the other had no weapon in his hand,
and knew that he could trust him.

Today, we don't carry swords,
but shaking hands can still mean "You can trust me."
Men and women often shake hands now as a friendly gesture
that means "How nice to meet you" or "It's good to see you again"
or "Welcome" or "Goodbye, and I hope we meet again."

THINGS THAT
GO TOGETHER

Composition is a big word
that's made from two smaller parts—
com-, which means "together,"
and *position*, which means "putting."
So *composition* means "together-putting"
or "something that has been put together."
Now you know what the word *composition* means.

Turn the next few pages to learn
how you or other people can put together,
or compose, things that you see
so that you can get certain meanings from them
just by looking at them.

It
Makes You
Wonder

When you look at this picture,
you must wonder what the artist means by it.
At first, many of the shapes look real.
But when you look again, they seem strange.
In fact, the more you look
at the shapes in the picture,
the stranger they get.

Are you looking at a picture of a dream
or a picture of a jumbled jungle scene?

No matter what you see in the picture,
and no matter how you feel about the picture,
you must wonder about it.
That's probably just why the artist
put together, or composed,
the many shapes the way he did.
He wants you to look, be surprised,
and then wonder about what you're looking at.

Nature at Daybreak
by Max Ernst

Have You Ever Made a Composition?

If you've read the first page in this section,
you know what the word *composition* means—
"together-putting" or "something that has been put together."
And since you've probably put lots of things together,
you, too, have made many compositions without even knowing it.

Do you know that you make a composition
when you put together, or draw,
the shapes and colors of a picture?

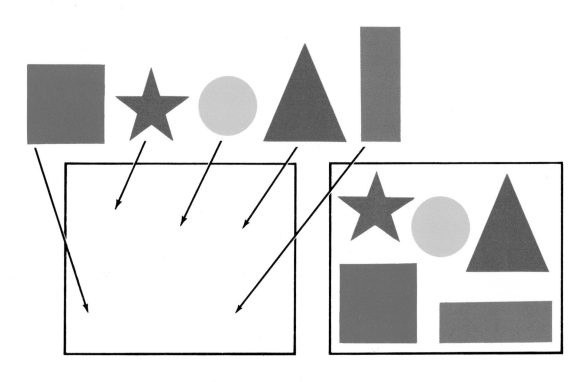

Do you know that you make a composition
when you put together, or write,
the words and sentences of a story?

Do you know that you make a composition
when you put together, or arrange,
the furniture in your room?

Do you know that you make a composition
whenever you put anything together
to make one main thing?—

Well, *now* you know.

SILENT CHEERS

At football games,
and other sports events,
people in the grandstand
can cheer for their team
without yelling.
They use cards.

Here's how they do it:
One part of the grandstand is saved
for students carrying big square cards.
One of the students signals the others
to hold up the first of their cards.
When the students
hold their number 1 cards over their heads,
the cards fit next to each other
and form a big picture.
The picture might show a tiger
or bicycle racers
or words like "GO, TEAM!"
Later, they use their other cards
to make other pictures.
The cards are like pieces of a puzzle.
When put together correctly,
they make the right picture.

Card section at a sporting event in Asia

Card section at an American football game

What
Scattered Stones
Can Mean

Suppose you are walking through a field one day, and you see a big stone. A little farther, you see another stone that looks a lot like the first one. You keep walking and seeing more and more of these stones that look so much alike.

You start to wonder if the stones mean something special. Maybe they mean more than just a lot of stones scattered in a field.

If you were an archaeologist (a person who studies ancient ruins), you might get into an airplane and fly over the stones. Some archaeologists study the arrangement of stones in ancient ruins from high in the sky, to see if the stones form a pattern.

An airplane view of stones in a field in Avebury, England,
shows what may have been a place of worship long ago.
The picture on the facing page
shows some of the stones up close.

And if the stones do form a pattern, it means that people prob-ably put them there long ago.

The next thing you'd do, if you were an archaeologist, would be to try to figure out what the ruins once were. Were the stones once part of an old town, an ancient wall, or a place where people used to worship? Study the picture and see if you can figure out what the stones once meant.

Patterns on Your Fingertips

THIS MEANS YOU—
if this is your fingerprint.
All fingerprints are patterns of lines
put together, or composed, something like this one.
But no two people in the whole world
have exactly the same composition of lines on their fingertips.
So the way the lines of a fingerprint
are put together, or composed, means
"this fingerprint belongs to one certain person, and no one else."

F.B.I. men, policemen, and military men
use fingerprints to identify people.
They keep copies of people's fingerprints.
When they are trying to identify a person,
they compare fresh fingerprints
with fingerprints they already have copies of.

If a fresh fingerprint matches
one of the fingerprints they have copies of,
they know they have found their man.
It couldn't be any other person because nobody else
has the same fingertip pattern.

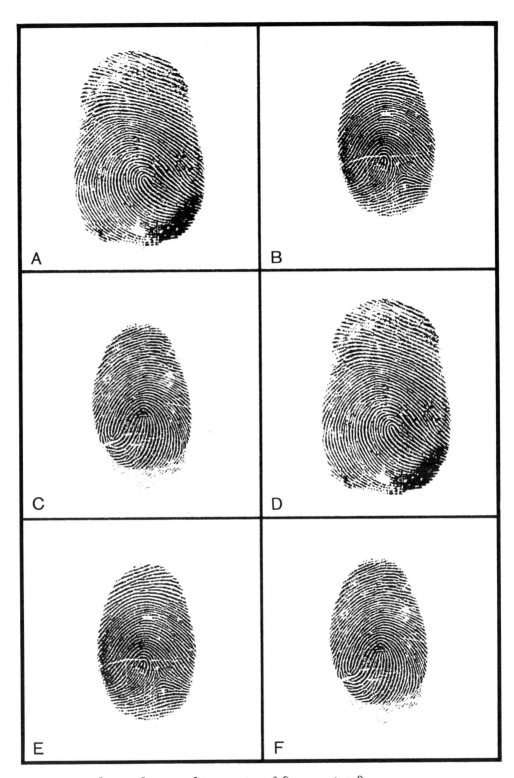

Can you pick out the matching pairs of fingerprints?
For answers see pages 312–313.

Putting the Right Note
in the Right Place

All those blobs, lines, ovals, dots, bars,
and tails scattered around don't mean a thing—
unless you put them together, or compose them in a certain way.

Now you can see that all these parts form musical notes.

This is a whole note.

This is a half note, which you sing
half as long as a whole note.

This is a dotted half note, which you sing
three-quarters as long as a whole note.

This is a quarter note, which you sing
only one-fourth as long as a whole note.

A little tail added to a quarter note
makes it an eighth note, which you sing
only one-eighth as long as a whole note.

But notes don't mean much unless you know
how high or low to sing or play them.
So they must be arranged, or composed,
on a musical staff, which looks like this:

You put high notes on this staff:

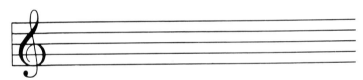

And you put low notes on this staff:

The higher the position of a note on a staff,
the higher you sing or play it.
The lower the position of a note on a staff,
the lower you sing or play it.

A person who puts musical notes together to make music
is called a composer.
When a composer composes a song,
he must know which note to put where,
so that his musical composition will mean
what he wants it to mean.

The Case of the Missing Hot Dog

It happened about noon one muddy spring morning. Mrs. Roberts was coming up the basement stairs when she heard the sound of feet scampering out the back door. When she entered the kitchen, she saw muddy footprints on the floor . . . and one of the hot dogs was missing from the counter. She wasn't angry about the floor, because it was dirty anyway. But the boys knew they weren't supposed to eat just before lunch. She opened the back door and called to Johnny and Mike.

"How many times have I told you not to eat before lunch?"

"I didn't eat anything, Mom," said Johnny.

"I didn't either!" chimed in Mike.

Mrs. Roberts frowned at the boys. "Then what were you doing in the kitchen just now?"

"Well, we were getting kinda hungry, so we thought we'd look around for a snack. But we ran outside when we heard you coming up the stairs. That's all, Mom. Honest," Johnny pleaded.

"That's strange," said Mrs. Roberts. "Then who took the hot dog?"

She turned and looked again at the position of the footprints on the kitchen floor. For the first time she saw that none of the footprints led to the counter where the hot dogs were. So the hot dog must have been taken by someone—or something—too clean to leave any footprints. There was just one creature who could have done it.

Mrs. Roberts went into the living room. There sat Rufus, the cat, licking his whiskers. Then Mrs. Roberts knew. She smiled to herself as she looked at the cat, who was much too clean to make any footprints. "All sorts of mysteries have been solved," she thought, "by detectives who study the composition of footprints left by the criminal at the scene of a crime. But I wonder how many times the composition of footprints has shown who *didn't* do it."

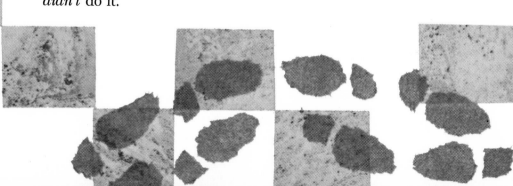

The Highest
Building
in Town

At one time, churches in Europe
were the biggest, highest buildings in town.
They were so high
that people could see them from miles away.
Churches were also in the center of town,
or very close to the center,
so that the other buildings in town
were never very far from the church.
Many of these big, tall churches
are called cathedrals.

People had a reason for building
their huge cathedrals in the center of town.
The cathedral was a symbol
of God, religion, and church.
People felt close to God
because they knew they were
close to their cathedral.
And they were reminded of God
even when they were far from town,
because they could see their cathedral
from miles away.

If you were to see a cathedral town—
put together, or composed,
with a huge, old cathedral in the center—
you'd see that God, religion, and church
were very important to the people
who lived there.

The Adoration of the Magi by Sandro Botticelli

Look Here!

A lot of people would look right at the middle of this picture.
In fact, that's where the artist wants you to look,
and he did everything he could to make sure you would look
right at the middle.

He painted an old ruined doorway
around the Mother and Child,
to draw your attention to them.
Many of the people in the picture
are looking at the same place,
so that you must be curious
to see what they're looking at.
They're looking at the Mother and Child,
who are right in the middle of the picture.

Now look at the same picture with your eyes partly closed.
Can you see that many of the people in the picture
are arranged in an X-shaped pattern?

And the artist placed Mother and Child
right in the middle, where the two lines of the X cross.
So you see, the artist put together,
or composed, the parts of his picture
so that people would be sure to look where he wanted them to.
This is a composition that makes you look right at the middle.

An artist can make you look at other parts of a picture, too,
just by the way he arranges, or composes,
the shapes in his picture.

Where do you suppose the artist
who composed this picture wants you to look?

Jockeys in the Rain by Edgar Degas

Portrait of Cornelius Van der Geest by Sir Anthony Vandyke

Light and Dark

What's the first thing you see when you look at this picture?
You probably see the man's light face,
because that's the only light spot in the picture.

The light face surrounded by dark colors
means that the artist wants you to look at the face.
The artist planned this composition so that the light face
would stand out from the rest of the picture.
He put together, or composed, the colors
so that they would show off
the most important part of his composition.

Poster for Aristide Bruant by Henri de Toulouse-Lautrec

An artist can do just the opposite, too.
He can show off something that is very dark
by surrounding it with light-colored paint.
A dark object surrounded by light paint
means that the artist wants you to look at the dark shape.

129

The Golden Rectangle

A very special shape that some artists use when they paint
a picture, and some architects use when they plan buildings,
looks like this: ▭
They call it a golden rectangle.
Of course, the rectangle doesn't really have a golden color.
Artists probably call it golden
because, to them, its shape is as special as gold.

You can see the shape of the golden rectangle
in many buildings and paintings.

The white lines
in this picture
form a golden rectangle.

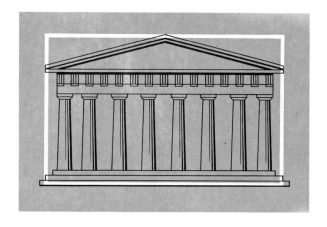

The golden rectangle
may have been used
to design the shape
of this famous building
from ancient Greece,
the Parthenon.

A golden rectangle was added to the doorway in this famous painting called **The Bedroom.** The artist, Pieter de Hooch, may have used the rectangle in planning his painting.

Here's how you can compose your own golden rectangle.
Draw a square with a line down the center.
Then take a compass and put the sharp point at A.
Draw part of a circle from B to C,
and extend the bottom line of the square to C.
Then extend the top line of the square
so that it's as long as the bottom line is.
Now draw a line to connect the top and the bottom lines,
and there's your own golden rectangle!
You can use it, if you want to, to put together,
or compose, your own pictures.

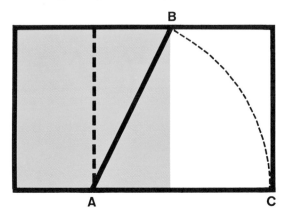

Position Means Meaning

You can change the meaning of each of these words.
Just change the position of letters in each word
to make another word with a different meaning.
The pictures give you hints. For answers see pages 312–313.

You give words meaning by the way you compose the letters.

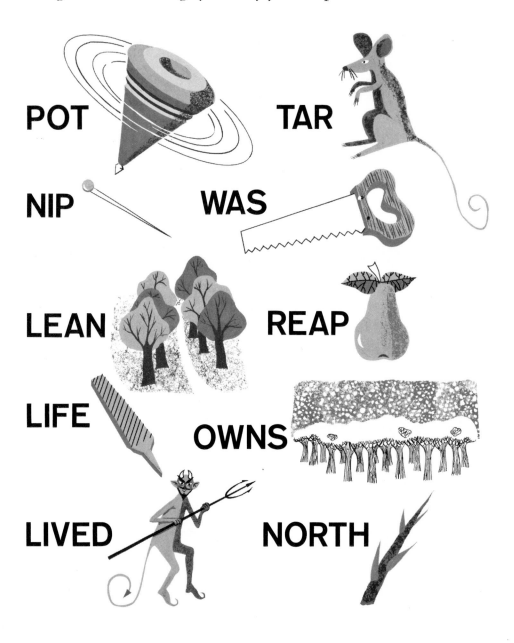

POT

TAR

NIP

WAS

LEAN

REAP

LIFE

OWNS

LIVED

NORTH

CLOTHES AND TRIMMINGS

You can tell many things about people just by looking
at the clothes and trimmings they wear.
Without any words—
their clothes and trimmings can mean
that the people are from a certain part of the world.
Without any words—
their clothes and trimmings can mean
that the people do a certain kind of work.
Without any words—
their clothes and trimmings can also mean
bravery, power, authority, or *good luck.*

On the next few pages you can find out
what some kinds of clothes and trimmings mean.

The Clothes They Wear

An artist can tell you something about
the people in the pictures he paints
by the clothes he shows them wearing.
What do the clothes tell you
about the women in these pictures?

Anne of Cleves
by Hans Holbein the Younger

Old Woman with Rosary ▶
by Paul Cézanne

135

Dancing Costumes

Sometimes the costume you wear
means that you're a certain kind of dancer.

If I wore this costume
and I were a dancer,
what kind of dancer would I be?
I'd be a cossack dancer,
because I'd be wearing a special hat,
coat, and boots.

If I wore this costume
and I were a dancer,
what kind of dancer would I be?
I'd be a ballerina,
because I'd be wearing a tutu.

If I wore this costume
and I were a dancer,
what kind of dancer would I be?
I'd be a flamenco dancer,
because I'd be wearing flowers in my hair,
and a flounced dress.

If I wore this costume
and I were a dancer,
what kind of dancer would I be?
I'd be a hula dancer,
because I'd be wearing a grass skirt.

MacKellar

Barclay

MacBean

Tartans Tell a Story

Long ago weavers in Scotland designed tartan plaids
for most of the important families there.
The weavers kept careful records
of the design of every plaid they made.
The plaid for each family
had to be basically the same,
but sometimes a few extra lines were added
for important people in the family.

You can see the different tartan plaids
in pictures of Scottish people
wearing short, pleated skirts, called kilts.

If you know the meaning of the tartan plaids,
you can tell
    what part of Scotland the Scotsmen come from,
    what families they belong to,
    and how important they are.

Stewart, Dress   Elliot   Menzies, Dress

Suits Made of Metal

Here is a skull, or helmet
with a visor.

Here are a helmet and visor
with a gorget, or collar.

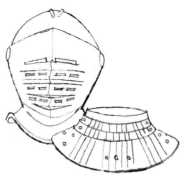

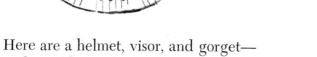

Here are a helmet, visor, and gorget—
with pauldrons, or shoulder pieces.

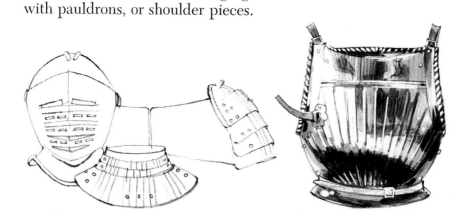

Here are a helmet, visor, gorget, and pauldrons—
with a breastplate.

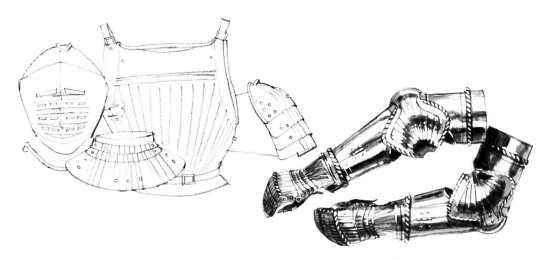

Here are a helmet, visor, gorget, pauldrons, and breastplate—
with couters, vambrace, and gauntlets, or arm pieces and gloves.

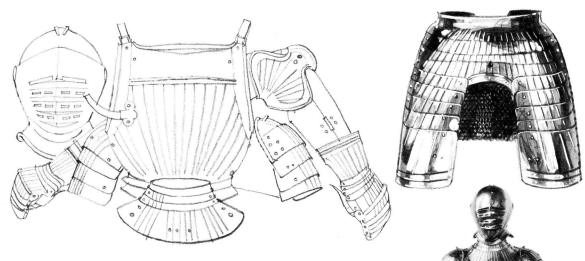

Here are a helmet, visor, gorget, pauldrons, breastplate,
couters, vambrace, and gauntlets—
with tasses, or a skirt.

Here are a helmet, visor, gorget, pauldrons,
breastplate, couters, vambrace,
gauntlets, and tasses—
with cuisses, poleyns, greaves,
and sabatons, or leg pieces and shoes.

Put them all together and you have a suit of armor.
And suits of armor mean *knights*.
Long ago, knights wore suits of armor
to protect themselves in battle.

Here Comes the Bride

A long white dress, a flowing veil,
something old, something new,
something borrowed, something blue,
and a penny in her shoe—
all these things together mean *bride*.

Brides wear white
because white is supposed to mean joy and virtue.
The something old, new, borrowed, blue,
and the penny
are supposed to mean good luck.

The wearing of the bridal veil
may mean that the bride is protected from evil.
Or it may be a symbol of obedience,
because at the wedding
a bride sometimes promises
to love, honor, and obey her husband.

Clothes Can Show Where You're Going

If you wear play clothes,
it could mean you're going out to play.
If you wear school clothes,
it could mean you're going to school.
If you wear party clothes,
it could mean you're going to a party.

If your father wears a sport shirt,
trousers, and a sweater,
or some other kind of sports clothes,
it could mean he's going to play golf or go bowling.

If your father wears a suit,
a white shirt, and a tie,
or some other kind of work clothes,
it could mean he's going to work.

If your father wears a tuxedo,
or other party clothes,
it could mean he's going to a party.

The clothes that people wear often tell you
the kind of thing they are going to do.

Feathers in Their Bonnets

How did an Indian brave in certain tribes get a war bonnet?
He had to work for it.
Each feather in the bonnet
had to be earned in battle.
And each feather meant something.

A few strands of red horsehair on top of a feather
meant that the brave had killed an enemy.

A red feather with a notch in it
meant that the brave had scalped an enemy.

A feather that was split or dyed red
meant that the brave had been wounded.

The position of the feather meant something, too.

A feather standing straight up meant *brave deed*.

A tilted feather meant *less brave deed*.

A feather pointing straight down
meant *least brave deed*—but still brave.

A war bonnet,
like the one
the Cherokee warrior
wears in this picture,
used to be
a sign of great honor.
But today,
when an Indian
wears feathers,
he wears them
just for decoration.

147

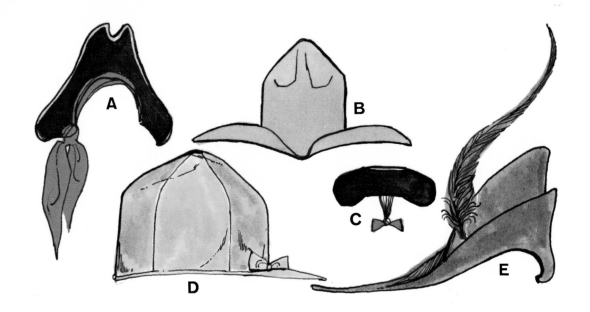

Hats and Shoes That Go Together

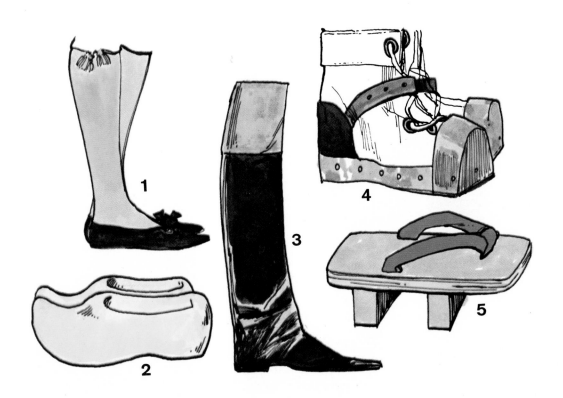

Some clothes go together.
And clothes that go together
make you think of a particular person, job, or country.

Can you match each hat at the top of these pages
with the correct pair of shoes at the bottom of these pages?

For answers see pages 312–313.

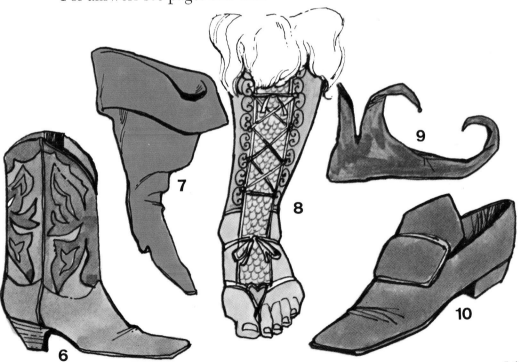

Where Did You Get That Hat?

Wearing a hat can mean lots of things.
But sometimes, a particular kind of hat
means that the person who wears it
comes from a certain country.

If I came from a country where girls wear fancy lace hats
perched on their heads,
where would I come from?
France—that's what a lacy hat
from a part of France called Brittany tells you.

If I came from a country where boys wear big hats
with wide brims that shade their faces,
where would I come from?
Mexico—that's what a sombrero tells you.

If I came from a country
where girls wear little white caps
with wings sticking out on the sides,
where would I come from?
The Netherlands—
that's what a Dutch winged cap tells you.

If I came from a country where men wear hats
with tassels and no brims,
where would I come from?
Turkey, Egypt, or North Africa—that's what a fez tells you.

If I came from a country where men and boys wear long scarfs
wrapped around their heads
and tucked in here and there,
where would I come from?
India—that's what a turban tells you.

151

They All Mean "Cowboy"

Levis and chaps,
broad-brimmed hats,
high-heeled boots,
and bandanas
mean *cowboys*.

Baggy trousers,
bright scarfs,
and wide silver belts
mean *cowboys*, too—
but, in Argentina
and Uruguay,
these cowboys
are called *gauchos*.

Flat-topped hats,
short capes,
leggings with fringes,
and high-heeled boots
mean *cowboys,* too—
but, in Chile,
these cowboys are called *huasos.*

Real Clothes
for Make-Believe People

Sometimes you can tell the characters in stories
just by the clothes they wear.

A black mask, a white horse, a white hat, and silver bullets?

Red boots and cape, and a blue leotard with a big red "S" on it?

A curved pipe, a hunting cap, and a cape-like coat?

"Hi yo, Silver! Away!"
It's the Lone Ranger!

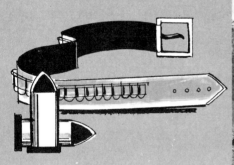

"It's a bird! It's a plane! No, it's Superman!"

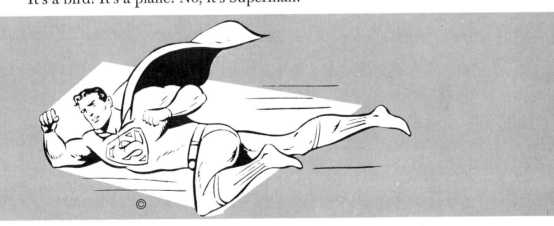

"Elementary, my dear Watson." It's Sherlock Holmes!

A Ring Can Mean Forever

A ring is a circle,
and a circle sometimes means *eternity*—
time that never ends.
A circle can mean eternity
because you can't find
the beginning or end of the line
that makes a circle.

Wedding ring

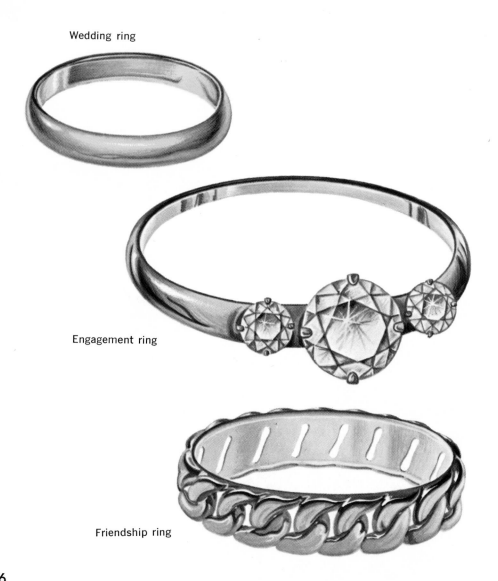

Engagement ring

Friendship ring

156

What Do Birthstone Rings Mean?

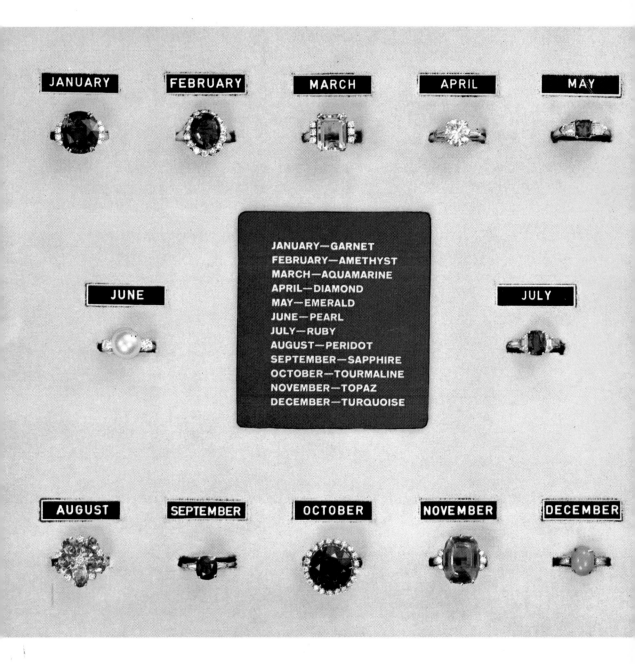

JANUARY—GARNET
FEBRUARY—AMETHYST
MARCH—AQUAMARINE
APRIL—DIAMOND
MAY—EMERALD
JUNE—PEARL
JULY—RUBY
AUGUST—PERIDOT
SEPTEMBER—SAPPHIRE
OCTOBER—TOURMALINE
NOVEMBER—TOPAZ
DECEMBER—TURQUOISE

Many people wear a birthstone ring
to show which month they were born in.
Which one of these birthstones stands for the
month you were born in?

Imperial Crown of Russia

Historic crown of the Holy Roman Empire

Crown of King Christian IV of Denmark

Historic Iron Crown of Lombardy

Royal crowns
of Greece were used
at the wedding ceremony
of Prince Juan Carlos
of Spain and his bride,
Princess Sophia of Greece.

All Kinds of Crowns

The word "crown" can mean many things.
"Crown" can mean *head*,
   the *top*, or highest point,
   part of a hat, part of a tooth, a silver coin,
   and the tip of a deer's horn.

The words "The Crown" can mean the *king* or *queen*.
And the crown that a king or queen wears
is a symbol of power and authority.

Court Jester

Multicolored pants and shirt,
a cap with dangling, jingling, jangling bells,
shoes with curved-up toes and bells at the tips—
these clothes and trimmings meant that the man who wore them
was a court jester.

A court jester was like a clown.
But a court jester told his jokes and stories
and did his dancing and prancing for the king and queen
and other members of a royal court.
Besides telling jokes and dancing,
he took part in family gatherings,
played with the children,
and sometimes he even gave advice to the king.

Jester by William Merritt Chase ▶

State trooper

Royal Canadian Mounted Policeman

A Belt With a Man's Name

If you see someone wearing a belt
that looks something like this,
it could mean
    that he goes to a military school,
    that he is a military policeman,
    that he is a state trooper,
    or that he is a Royal Canadian Mounted Policeman.
This special belt is called a Sam Browne belt.
Even school crossing guards wear a belt
that looks a little like the Sam Browne belt.

General Samuel Browne

General Pershing wearing
a Sam Browne belt

A British general, Samuel Browne,
designed the belt to carry his sword and pistol.
The first belt had two shoulder straps—
one to support the weight of the sword
and the other to support the weight of the pistol.

During World War I, the Sam Browne belt
had a special meaning to soldiers.
When the soldiers saw the belt on a man
in the United States Army or the United States Marine Corps,
they knew that he was an officer, not an enlisted man.

School crossing guards

A Sword Is More Than A Weapon

A sword is a weapon.
But it also has some special meanings.
A sword means *power* and *authority*.
The sword that is given to a king when he is crowned
is a symbol of the king's power and authority in the land.

Another time a sword has meaning
is when a king uses it to make someone a knight.
When a king makes a man into a knight,
he taps the man on the shoulder with the sword and says,
"I dub you knight."
The sword is a symbol of knighthood
and of the knight's power and authority.

Still another time a sword has meaning
is when an army officer uses it.
Nowadays, officers sometimes wear swords for decoration.
But years ago, when an officer gave up his sword after a battle,
it meant that he surrendered all his power and authority.

This picture shows how a king of long ago
used a sword to dub a man into knighthood.

164

WHAT MODELS
STAND FOR

Without words—
models tell us about things that are
    too big to see
    or too little to see
    or don't exist anymore
    or haven't been made yet.
When we want to see what something is like,
but we can't see the real thing,
we make a model to take its place.

The next few pages will tell you
how models can mean something.

Photographs as Models

At first glance,
this picture might look like blobs of colors.
But compare the painting with the photograph.
Can you see how the artist used the photograph
as one of many such models for the painting?

Photograph of Humberto Moro

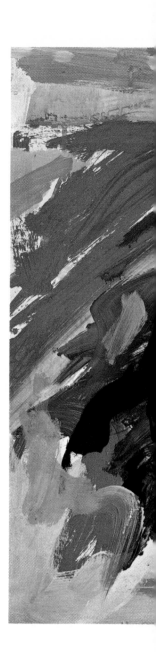

Tijuana by Elaine de Kooning

Walter Netsch, architect, looks at a model that he designed
for the University of Illinois Chicago Circle Campus.

City on a Table

Where should the new highway be built?
The city officials couldn't decide.
Then one official said,
"Let's take a helicopter, and fly over the city.
In that way, we can see the whole city at once,
and we can plan a route for the new highway."
But the mayor reminded them
that the city didn't own a helicopter.
"Besides," he continued, "what we really need is a man
who knows how to make improvements in a city.
I'm going to call in a city planner.
He can plan a good route for the highway,
and maybe come up with some other improvements, too.
What's more, he'll show us what they look like
on a model of the city."

When a city planner suggests changes, he wants to show
what the city would look like if certain changes were made.
So, he can prepare a small model
that shows the city—and the changes.

The model may show a new highway or a new park
or new buildings before they are built.
If the city officials approve the changes in the model city,
then work can begin on the changes in the real city.

This photograph shows the real Circle Campus.

Bones from a skeleton of a giant land sloth

Foot bones of a horned dinosaur

Skeleton of a duckbilled dinosaur

Skeleton of the giant dinosaur, Gorgosaurus

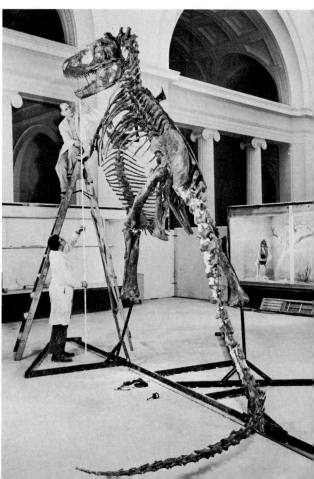

Bringing Back the Dinosaur

Dinosaurs were terrifying monsters!
Some grew as tall as trees,
and some had teeth the size of daggers.
But you can't see any real dinosaurs today.
They disappeared from the earth long before any men lived.
So how do we know what the dinosaurs were like?
We make models of them.
Model dinosaurs look almost as terrifying as real ones.
They are bigger than elephants
and they have a grey-green skin that's thick and rough.
And some models even move and roar.
But how do we know the models are like the real ones?
Scientists study the bones of dinosaurs
that have been dead for millions and millions of years.
From their studies, they can make very accurate guesses
about what the real dinosaurs looked like.

Then workers spend many weeks building model dinosaurs of
   clay and canvas,
   plaster and pipe,
   wire and stone,
and even parts of the ancient, real dinosaur bones.
You can see model dinosaurs in museums of natural history,
or in movies about dinosaurs.

The dinosaur, Tyrannosaurus, from a painting called
Tyrannosaurus and Triceratops by C. R. Knight

Almost Like Being There

Deep in the cave, by the dim light of the fire,
we see cavemen chipping tools from a large stone.
But how can this be?
There aren't any cavemen today.

We're looking at a diorama in a history museum.
This diorama was made by museum workers
who gathered all the facts they could find about cavemen.
Then, they built models
of trees, bushes, rocks, and of people long ago,
and blended them with a carefully painted background.
The diorama is the most realistic picture of cavemen we can get.
Dioramas can show scenes about many times in history,
or scenes about many ways people live.

A model of an atom is thousands of times larger than a real atom.

A model
of the solar system
is thousands of times
smaller than
the solar system.

Too Tiny and Too Big

No matter how hard you tried,
you would never be able to find a photograph
showing all the parts of an atom.
Atoms are too tiny.
And you would never be able to find a photograph
showing all the parts of the solar system, either.
The solar system is too big.
From studying and experimenting, scientists have a good idea
of what the atom and the solar system look like.

So scientists and science teachers can use models
to show what an atom or the solar system looks like.

It's interesting that the model of an atom
and the model of the solar system
look something alike.

An army engineer uses a model to explain the Dardanelle Lock and Dam for the
Arkansas River, Arkansas.

A Model for Making Sure

You just can't be too careful when you're going to build a dam.

No one knows this better than the engineers who have to do it.
They may plan to build a dam that will
span a mile-wide river valley, stand as tall as ten houses,
and hold back a large lake.
The equipment and material alone will cost
millions and millions of dollars.
And it will take many years to finish the job.
The engineers just can't afford to make any mistakes.
But how can the engineers be sure
that everything will be as right as is possible
before they start to work?

They can build a model of the dam that looks and works
just like the real dam they want to build.
The model dam is much smaller and it costs a lot less.
If the model works, the engineers can be pretty sure
that the real one will work, too.

This is how the real Dardanelle Lock and Dam looks.

Flying Nowhere

"FIVE . . . FOUR . . . THREE . . . TWO . . . ONE . . .
LIFTOFF!"

The astronauts begin their long space journey.
But how can the astronauts know what to do,
if they've never flown in outer space before?

They practice for months—even years—
in special training machines.
These machines are really models.
They show the astronauts what space flight will be like,
even though they never leave the ground.

Inside the model, the astronaut sees
instruments that show the same kinds of things
that instruments in a real space capsule
on a real space flight would show.
When the countdown begins, the astronaut is ready—
thanks to the model.

Before astronauts make a space flight, they get special training in models
of space capsules, like the model of a Gemini spacecraft in this picture.

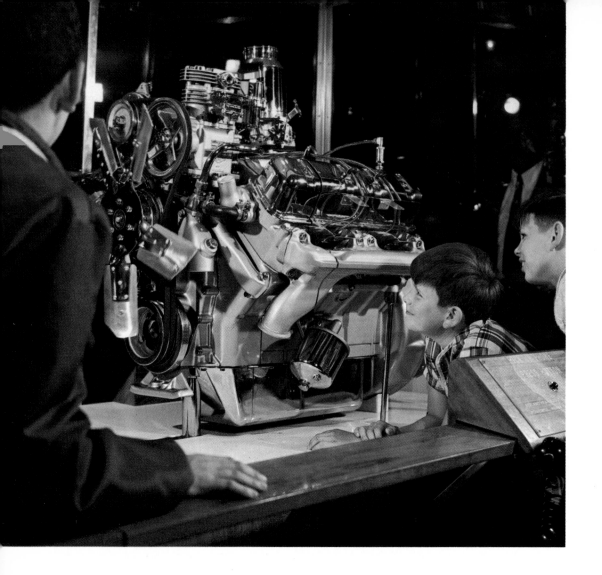

Looking Through a Machine

"If I could just see how that car engine works!"
Johnny wants to see how the gasoline gets to the carburetor
and how the pistons move up and down in the cylinders.
He wants to see through all the parts of the engine.
But the engine is covered with solid metal.
He can't see through metal.
So, he needs a cutaway model.

Cutaway models of engines are like real engines.
But the models are uncovered
so that you can see all the parts.
Some parts are made of clear plastic or glass
so that you can see what happens
inside the tubes and chambers of the engines.

You can see all kinds of machines in cutaway models,
from automobile engines and farm machines,
to watches, telephones, and telescopes.

Children in the picture at the left look at a model engine of a truck.
The picture below shows children looking at the same model
with its outer covering removed.

Better Than People

Dummies help people—
that is, dummies that are models.
Dummies that are models
sometimes take the place of real people.

Men who own clothing stores use dummies to show
what the clothes they sell would look like on real people.
No live model could stand in one place
all night and all day, everyday.
But store dummies can.

Dummies are also used for jobs that are too dangerous for people.
Engineers use dummies when they test safety devices for cars.
They put dummies into the cars, and crash the cars into each other.
Then, they examine the dummies to see
how badly real people might have been hurt.

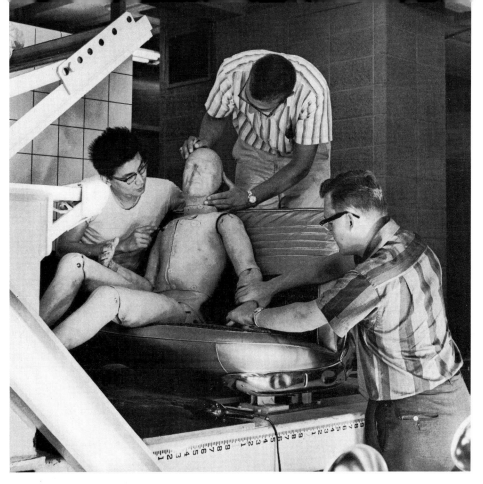

Engineers use a dummy with machines mounted inside it when they test an automobile for safety.

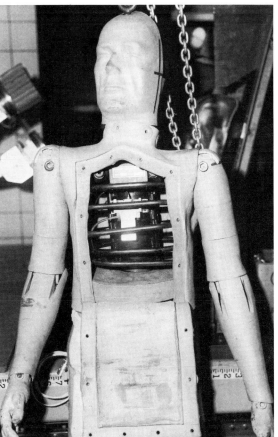

183

United States Marines study a model battle zone set up in a gymnasium.

A Model Battle Zone

"Attack with full force!
First, soften the area with big guns.
Then, send in tanks and infantry . . ."

The men listen carefully as they study the plan of battle.
One man puts model ships, planes, cannons, tanks, trucks,
and soldiers into place in the model battle zone.
The men know that the battle isn't going to be real.
But they know that, someday, the battle could be real.
And they know that the model battle zone
will help them practice and be ready for any real battle.

In many military training schools, the officers and men
use model battlefields and model battle zones
to study how to plan a battle.
The model battle zones look like real battle zones, only smaller.
They show ridges, ditches, gullies, and many other features
that the officers and men might see in a real battle zone.
What the men learn from studying a model battle zone might help them
to win a battle—or even a war—in a real battle zone.

Officers inspect a model of a battle zone.

A Korean officer shows a United States officer a model of a firing range.

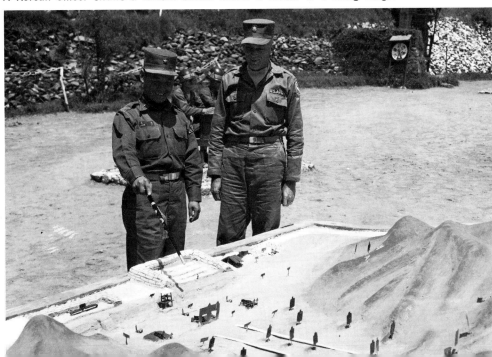

Actors spend a lot of time practicing in their everyday clothes on a plain, undecorated stage.

Before the Play Begins

What a mess!
From the first day of rehearsals for the play,
the director didn't know what he wanted the actors to do.
His biggest problem was changing his mind
about where he wanted the actors to be.
The actors grew more and more confused.
Finally, the rehearsals were cancelled,
and so was the play.

How could the director have known ahead of time
where he wanted the actors to be?

He could have made his plans with the help of a model stage.

Then, before rehearsals began, he could have moved
model figures around the model stage,
until he had the action the way he wanted it.

This model stage not only has model actors, but model logs,
model scenery, and model bridge, as well.

This is how the real stage looks during an actual performance of a play.

Statues Can Be Models

Some sculptors are model builders.
They don't make model cars
or model planes or model trains.
They make models of people,
and they call them *statues*.

Sometimes, the statue-models
are the same size as real people.
Other times, they're a lot larger than real people.
But if a sculptor makes a statue, a model of someone,
you can be sure that someone is worth remembering.

The famous storyteller, Hans Christian Andersen, and the swan
from his story, "The Ugly Duckling," were the subjects for this statue.

MATERIALS CAN "TALK"

Materials are what things are made of.
    Paper is a material.
    Cotton, fur, gold,
    feathers, marble, parchment
are a few of the many different kinds of materials.
Sometimes—without a word being spoken—
you can look at a material and know what it means
and what it's used for.
Other times you can't tell by looking
and you have to learn what the material means.

You can find out what some materials mean, and why,
on the next few pages.

Boards, Stones, and Bones

Some artists make pictures out of
boards and stones and dried-out bones,
scraps of cloth,
bits of paper,
pieces of string and other things.

They use hammers and nails
and glue, too,
so that their pictures won't fall apart.

How many different things
and kinds of material
can you find in this picture?

Merz Construction
by Kurt Schwitters

Glass for Gold

Gold birds,
big disks of gold and silver the size of cartwheels,
a jeweled gold mask,
a helmet full of gold dust—
these were the kinds of gifts
the Aztec Indian Emperor,
Montezuma II,
sent to the Spanish soldier, Cortes,
when Cortes first landed in Mexico.

Cortes and his men were pleased with the gifts.
They knew that if they had discovered a land
where gold and silver were easy to find,
they would all be rich.
But first, they must give gifts to the Emperor in return.

What could they give
that would match the marvelous gifts they got?

192

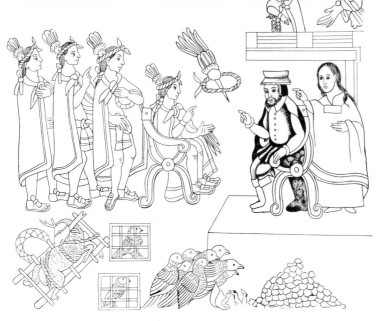

Cortes meets Montezuma in Tenochtitlán, later known as Mexico City.

The Aztec treasures
in the pictures below
are like those that
Montezuma gave to Cortes.

Surprisingly, all Cortes gave Montezuma
were some ordinary glass beads and some simple toys—
no better than the kind of things
you can buy in the dime store today.

You might think that Montezuma was insulted
when he got cheap glass beads for gold.
But he wasn't. He was delighted.
He had never seen glass before and he liked the beads.

Any kind of material—
gold or glass, silver or tin,
diamond or sea shell—
can be valuable if you think it is.

The Houses of
the Three Little Pigs

That wolf in the story "The Three Little Pigs," wasn't very smart.
If he had been human, he wouldn't have wasted so much time.
He would have just looked at the three houses—
one of straw, one of sticks, and one of brick,
and he would have known
that he couldn't blow down the brick house.

When we see houses or anything else
made of some kinds of materials,
like brick, stone, steel, or concrete,
we can know just by looking—without any words—
that they are probably strong and won't blow down easily.

And we don't even have to look at straw
to know it won't make a strong house.

Come to think of it, the first two pigs
weren't any smarter than the wolf, were they?

Tons of concrete were used to build this skyscraper.
One reason it looks strong is that we know concrete is strong.

Newsprint and Parchment

Most newspapers are printed
on a soft, cheap paper called newsprint.
The kind of paper that the news is printed on
is cheap so that you don't have to pay much
for your newspaper every day.
If you want to, you can read a newspaper
and then throw it away.
We're so used to cheap newspapers
that just by looking at paper like newsprint
we know that it's cheap and that we don't have to save it.

But there's another kind of paper
that's just the opposite.
You know just by looking at it
that you shouldn't throw it away.
This paper makes what is printed on it look important.
This important-looking paper is called parchment paper.
Real parchment was once used for paper, but it is expensive
because it's made from the skin of a sheep or a goat.
Parchment paper looks just about like real parchment.
It lasts for years and years,
but it is not as expensive as parchment.
That's why important documents
like the diploma you get when you graduate from school,
are usually printed on parchment paper.
They're supposed to last a long time.

This famous document, the Declaration of Independence of the United States of America, was written on parchment so that it would last for a long time.

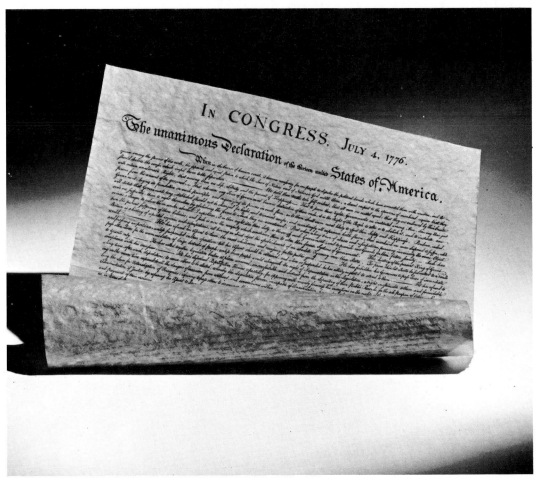

Leather jacket

Cotton shirt and shorts

Hot and Cold Clothes

Imagine wearing a fur coat in the summer sun,
or a seersucker sunsuit in the winter snow!
One way you'd be too hot. The other way you'd be too cold.
And either way, you'd look funny.

You can tell just by looking at the materials
that a fur coat isn't meant for summer wear,
and that a seersucker suit isn't made for winter wear.

Velvet dress

Wool sweater

Sunsuit

Cotton dress

Fur-trimmed parka

Straw hat

On these pages you see pictures of different clothes
made of different materials.
See if you can tell which are winter clothes,
and which are summer clothes.
For answers see pages 312–313.

Wool coat and muff

Bathing suit

199

Rubbers and Rubber Boots

When you see someone wearing rubbers or rubber boots,
you know he's going someplace
where his feet may get wet.
Even if you had never seen rubbers or rubber boots,
you might be able to guess what they were for—
just by looking.

Before boots made of rubber were invented,
people used to wear wooden shoes
or cork soled shoes in wet weather.
But rubbers and rubber boots
are much better to keep feet dry.
Someday, someone might find
something even better than rubbers or rubber boots
to keep your feet dry.
Perhaps some scientist will invent a plastic
to spray over your regular shoes.
Then no one would know whether or not
you're planning to go out in the rain.
But until that time,
rubbers and rubber boots still mean
that whoever wears them
is probably going somewhere that's wet.
You don't need words or talk
to guess what some materials mean.

Paperbacks and Hardbacks

Nobody has to tell you.
You don't need a sign.
All you have to do
is look at the cover of a paperback book
next to the cover of a hardback book,
and you know that the paperback book
won't last as long.

There's an old saying that goes:
    "You can't tell a book by its cover."
That's true if you are talking about what's inside the book
and whether the book is a good one or not.
Many of the world's greatest books are in paperback covers,
and you could never say that a book was no good
just because it was in a paperback.

But you can say when you look at its cover
whether a book will last a long time or not.

Light as Aluminum

If your father buys a ladder at the hardware store,
you can almost be sure
that he'll choose an aluminum ladder,
instead of a wooden one.
Why?
Because aluminum is light,
and a lot easier to carry around than wood.
That's one reason why aluminum is used
to make so many things today.
No one has to tell you
   that a boat made of aluminum
   is lighter than a boat made of wood,
   or that furniture made of aluminum
   is lighter than furniture made of wood,
   or that pots and pans made of aluminum
   are lighter than pots and pans made of stone or iron.
Just by looking, you can "feel"
how much things made of aluminum will weigh.

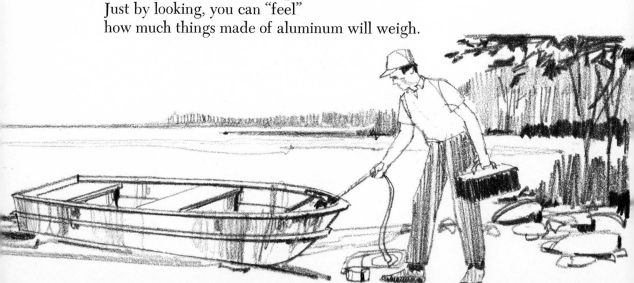

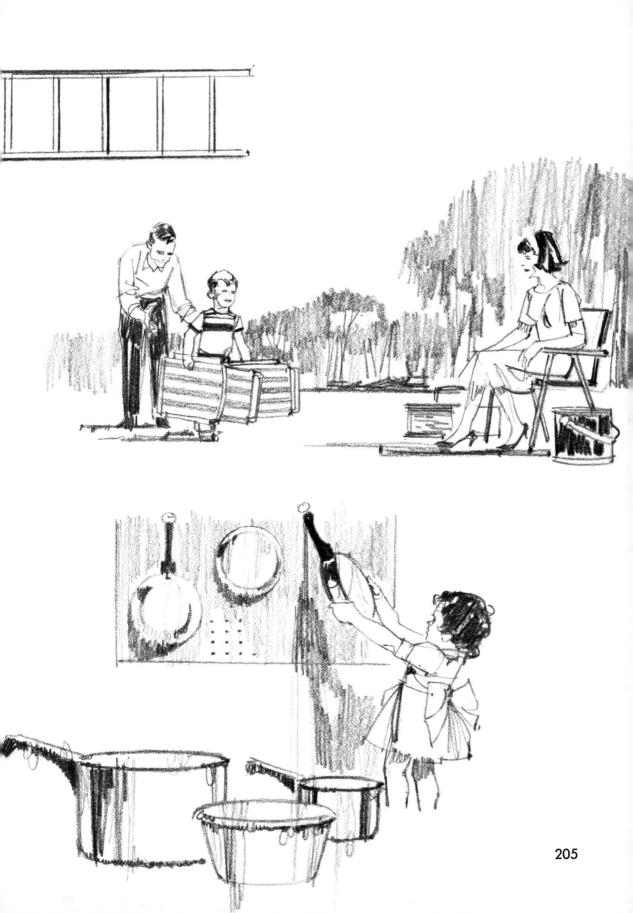

Stained Glass Windows

Sometimes windows are made of a glass you can't see through.
These are the windows made of stained glass
that you usually see in churches.
That's why you usually think of church
when you see stained glass windows.

Why are stained glass windows used mostly in churches?
Long ago the stained glass windows in churches
were like storybook pictures
that told the story of the Christian religion.
Many churches in Europe used them
even before North America was discovered.
Then churches in North America
used stained glass windows.

And even today,
if you see stained glass windows on a new building,
it would be a good guess that you're looking at a church.

A stained glass window ▶
in Coventry Cathedral, Coventry, England.

Field Museum of Natural History in Chicago, Illinois

Marble Pillars and Steel Stilts

Marble pillars look so strong
that you're not surprised when you see them
holding up the fronts
of some post offices, libraries, and banks.
But if you see skinny steel stilts
holding up a skyscraper,
you may wonder how it's possible.
Perhaps marble is stronger in some ways than steel.
Perhaps it isn't.
But why does marble *look* stronger?
Well, for one thing,
a steel stilt, or girder,
is usually not much bigger around than you are.
But when a marble pillar is used to hold up a building,
it may be ten times bigger around than you are.
And there's another reason
why marble may look stronger to us than steel.
No one used a steel girder for a building
until about eighty years ago.
We don't know of any very old steel girder buildings.
But the oldest marble columns we know of were built
more than two thousand years ago.
Marble looks stronger than steel to us
because we know it can stand for thousands of years.

An office building in Baltimore, Maryland,
designed by the architect Mies Van Der Rohe ▶

Be Careful

When you see a box
with a label on it saying, "GLASS—FRAGILE,"
you know that you had better not drop the box
for fear that you will break whatever is inside.
You need words to warn you.
But if you see a beautiful glass goblet,
nobody has to put the words "GLASS—FRAGILE"
on the goblet to warn you not to drop it.
You can tell that you shouldn't drop it
just by looking at the material it is made of—
glass.

THE PROPER PLACE

Settings are surroundings.
Everything we look at has something surrounding it,
even if the surroundings are only empty spaces.
Sometimes plain things can look beautiful
if we see them in a beautiful setting.
And sometimes fancy things can look plain—
depending on their setting.
People use settings
     to make things look different
     or to make fake things look real
     or to make things look special.

The next few pages will show you
many different kinds of settings
and what they can mean.

This house, designed by the architect Frank Lloyd Wright,
is called "Falling Water."
This is how "Falling Water" looks in the summertime.

Which Came First?

A famous architect designed this house.
The house and its setting
show how important one is to the other.
Do you think the architect planned the setting
to fit the house?
Or do you think he planned
the house to fit the setting?
Here's a clue.
The waterfall was part of the setting
before the house was built.

This is how "Falling Water" looks in the wintertime.

Store Windows

Most store owners show off the products they sell
in the windows of their stores.
But the store owner doesn't just dump the products
into the window any old way.
Instead, he carefully arranges
everything in the window into a certain setting,
so that shoppers will understand
what he wants them to know about his products.
A store owner can say different things
about his products by using different settings.

This setting tells shoppers that the many products
are being sold at low prices.

This setting tells shoppers that these products are special
and that no other products can compare with them.

Settings in a store window
also can help call shoppers' attention to a product.
Suppose the owner of a sporting goods store
wants to show off a new bicycle.
Which one of these settings does a better job?

Store owners use their windows to say a lot
about their products
without really saying a word.
It all depends on the setting they use.

Supermarket Settings

Groceries in a supermarket are arranged in settings
that attract shoppers' attention.
How does this work? Let's see.

"I think I'll stop at the supermarket for a quart of milk.
That's all I really need."

"Now how did I end up with all these things?
And I even forgot the milk!"

Here's how it happened. . . .

"These pineapples look so good,
I'll have to buy one
and fix it for lunch."

"A special on my favorite soup!"

"The lettuce and tomatoes look too good to pass up.
And that reminds me, I need salad dressing, too."

"Those lamb chops give me
an idea for dinner tonight."

Sometimes settings attract people so much
that they buy more than they planned to buy.

Dinner Is Served

"Mary, it's almost time for dinner. Set the table."

When Mary heard her mother remind her about her dinner-time job, she knew just what to do, because she set the table every night. And this is how the table looked when she finished setting it.

But the next evening, just as Mary started setting the table, the phone rang. It was her father calling to say he was bringing his boss home for dinner. So Mary's mother asked her to set the table in the special way that meant important company was coming. And this is how the table looked when she finished setting it.

Even though the food stays the same, a table setting can turn an ordinary family meal into a fancy dinner.

Going on Location

Long ago, when it wasn't so easy as it is today
to travel to faraway places, moviemakers had a problem.
Suppose they wanted to make a movie about Egypt.
To make the movie look as if it were taking place in Egypt,
the moviemakers had to build a fake Egyptian setting.
A fake setting was expensive and took a long time to build.
But if the moviemakers wanted Egyptian scenery,
they had to fake it.

Today, when moviemakers want to make a movie about Egypt,
they just go to Egypt instead of building a set.
Traveling in jet planes takes only a few hours
and not nearly so much money.
The director, actors, cameramen, and other workers
can travel to the real setting of the movie,
no matter where it is. When they go to the real setting,
they call it "going on location."

Compare the movie settings in the two pictures.
Which kind of movie would you rather see—
one with fake settings or real settings?

Landscaping: A Setting for a House

This is the Morgans' new house.
It has everything they've always wanted in a house—
fireplace, back porch, garage, even a basement recreation room.

But Mr. Morgan wasn't completely happy with the house.
He thought it needed a nicer setting.
So he went to work outside the house
and began to improve the setting.

There was so much work to do that he hired workmen to help him. And when they finished work outside, the house looked like this:

Notice how the setting improves the looks of the house.

A Dirty Old Baseball

If you found an old baseball all banged out of shape,
with its stuffing coming out,
you'd probably kick it aside and forget about it.
But if this were an important baseball—a famous baseball—
you'd probably put it in a place of honor
and show it off to everyone.

Well, that's just what some people have done
with certain baseballs, bats, gloves, and uniforms.
They've put them in a special setting—a place of honor.
The place is the National Baseball Hall of Fame and Museum.
You can visit this museum in Cooperstown, New York,
the town where baseball was invented.

Most of the things in the museum are old
and some of them are in poor condition.
But in the setting of a museum, they become important,
and people come from all over the world to see them.

This old baseball
is on display at the
Baseball Hall of Fame
in Cooperstown, New York.

Doubleday Field in Cooperstown, New York, used to be a cow pasture when Abner Doubleday, the inventor of baseball, played ball there more than a hundred years ago.

The last baseball autographed by Babe Ruth is displayed with other Babe Ruth souvenirs at the Hall of Fame.

Cy Young, one of baseball's greatest pitchers, gave a speech at the opening of a new section of the Hall of Fame in 1950.

Oklahoma! ▲

Cinderella ▲

H.M.S. Pinafore ▼

Curtain Going Up

When you go to a play,
as soon as the curtain goes up—even before the actors speak—
you know something about the play.
You know from the scenery on stage.
Scenery in a play is a setting
that tells you something about the characters.
The setting might tell you how they live or where they live
or what kind of work they do.

Look at the scenery,
then find the characters that belong in each setting.

Alice in Wonderland ▼

227

Outside view of the Cloisters

In Another World

Not far from some of the busiest streets
in one of the world's busiest cities,
you can take a trip back through time
more than seven hundred years,
into a European monastery that looks as if
it hasn't changed since it was first built.
It's almost as if you have taken a ride in a time machine.
But actually, all you have done is to step into a museum.

The Metropolitan Museum of Art in New York City
has a building called the Cloisters,
where many old paintings and statues are shown.
Most of these art works are about religious subjects.
At first most of them were kept in monasteries.
So when the museum directors collected these art works,
they built a monastery setting for them.
And today, when you walk through the Cloisters,
it's almost like journeying back in time to the real settings
where these paintings and statues first were seen.

The Spanish Room inside the Cloisters

A courtyard inside the Cloisters

Sports Settings

Football field

Baseball field

Boxing ring

Hockey rink

Basketball court

Every sport has to be played in a particular place
or on a particular kind of field.
This is the proper setting for the sport.
No other setting will do.

See if you can match each of the sports heroes below
with the setting in which he became famous.
For answers see pages 312–313.

Rocky Marciano   Jim Brown   Eddie Shore   Wilt Chamberlain   Ted Williams

Maurice Richard   Bob Cousy   Ty Cobb   John L. Sullivan   Red Grange

Sam Huff   Bobby Hull   Oscar Robertson   Willie Mays   Jack Dempsey

Mickey Mantle   Joe Louis   George Mikan   Otto Graham   Gordie Howe

The Innkeeper's Reward

Napoleon Bonaparte, Emperor of France, awoke, dressed, and went down the stairs of the inn where he and his generals had spent the night. Several of the generals were in the kitchen, and they jumped to attention and saluted when the emperor entered. The innkeeper and his wife were there, too. At first the innkeeper and his wife had been frightened, with the army of France camping in the fields surrounding their inn and with the emperor himself staying in their house. They knew that the emperor was a man with a terrible temper.

But now he was leaving.

The emperor accepted a cup of coffee from the innkeeper and said, "You have been a good host. I wish to reward you. Name your prize and it shall be yours."

These words astonished the innkeeper. He had expected no payment. Now he was afraid.

"If I ask for too much," the innkeeper thought, "he will become angry and perhaps punish us. If I ask for something he cannot give us, this too will anger him."

"What is your choice?" asked Napoleon.

"Your excellency, our needs are few and we have all that we want. It has been our pleasure to serve you. We want no reward."

"But I insist on paying you! Name your prize!" Napoleon demanded.

"Your excellency, we want nothing. But if you would reward us, perhaps you will do so by telling us something, instead of giving us something."

"What is it?" Napoleon asked.

"We have heard that when you were in Russia, the Russians captured the farmhouse where you were sleeping and that you hid up the chimney while they searched for you," said the innkeeper. "We would consider it a reward if you would tell us how you felt while the Russians were searching for you."

As the innkeeper finished his request, he looked at Napoleon and was terrified by what he saw! There was an expression of wild anger on the emperor's face. He motioned toward two of his men, and then pointed to the door. The soldiers stepped forward, grabbed the innkeeper and his wife and marched them out to the stable yard.

The soldiers dragged the innkeeper and his wife to one end of the stable yard and stood them against the wall. The innkeeper began to plead.

"Please your excellency, have mercy on us. I meant no harm. I am sorry for what I said. Please . . . If you must kill me, spare my wife for our children's sake." And while he said this, his wife moaned helplessly.

The emperor stood motionless while the soldiers tied the hands of the innkeeper and his wife behind their backs.

The soldiers marched away a few paces, and the innkeeper saw them raise their guns and get ready to fire. Then Napoleon spoke.

"Ready!" he called to the soldiers.

"Aim!" he said, and the innkeeper's wife screamed.

"Stop!" cried the emperor. And with that he marched over to the prisoners.

"Now," he said, "you know how I felt while the Russians were searching for me."

MORAL: Sometimes you can't understand how other people feel unless you're put in a similar setting.

Take Another Look

Something in this setting doesn't belong here.
You might not notice it at first.
But, when you do see it,
you will know it doesn't belong in this setting.
Just one misplaced thing is enough to spoil a setting.

How many misplaced things can you find in this setting?
For answers see pages 312–313.

SPECIAL MARKS

Marks that mean something special
are called symbols.
They look like scratches and squiggles.
But when you use them as symbols,
they stand for words and ideas,
and they help you save time and space.

On the next few pages
you will find out about
the meaning of some special marks and symbols
that are used in all kinds of work,
from cartoons to chemistry.

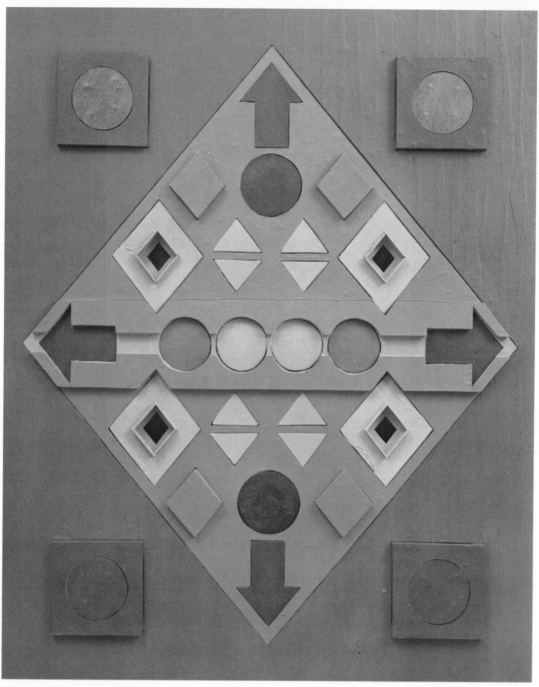

Blue Diamond by George Ortman

Symbols in Art

What do the signs and symbols
in this picture mean?
How do they make you feel?
Here, in this work of art, they can mean anything
you want them to.

A. DAIGGER & COMPANY
CHEMICALS

INDUSTRIAL & MARINE HARDWARE

SPAULDING & COMPANY

ANTIQUE MARKET Ltd.
WHOLESALE & RETAIL

GUIDARELLI NUT CO.
SHELLED & SALTED NUTS
WHOLESALE ★ ★ ★

And and &

What do these signs have in common?
At first, they all seem different.
But look carefully.
Each one has this mark in it: &
What does the symbol "&" mean?
And how did it come about?

At one time the symbol "&" was part of the English alphabet.
When children recited the alphabet and came to "&,"
they would say "and per se and."
That was a fancy way of saying,
"the sign for *and* in itself means and."

The symbol "&" isn't part of the English alphabet any more.
But we still have the symbol.
We no longer call the symbol "and per se and," though.
Now we squeeze the fancy phrase and just say "ampersand."
& is the way the symbol usually looks in print.
But sometimes, in print, it looks other ways.
And when people write it, it can look still other ways.
But all the shapes are ampersands.
We use them when we want to save space.
And they are all symbols that mean "and."

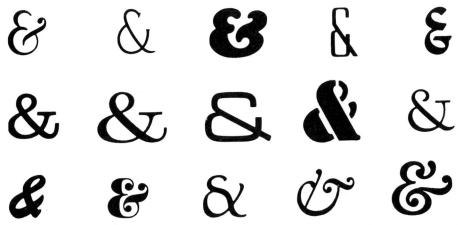

Cartoon Talk

Even though pictures don't move or talk,
a cartoonist can use special marks
to tell us that something is happening in cartoons.

When you see this mark around the words in a cartoon,
you know that the words inside the circle
are spoken by the cartoon character that the tail points to.
Cartoonists call this circle a balloon.

This kind of balloon means the words inside are being
thought—not spoken—by the character.

This kind of balloon means that the words inside
are coming over the telephone or the radio.

This means the character is running.

This means the character is shaking or shivering.

This means the character has an idea.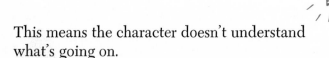

This means the character doesn't understand
what's going on.

This means something is shiny.

This means the character is falling in love.

And this means the character is sad or gloomy.

By using these special scratches and squiggles,
cartoonists tell you a lot—even when they don't use words.

BRICKMAN

H$_2$O Means Water

"Please pass the **H$_2$O**.
I put too much **NaCl** on my meat.
If I don't stop eating so much,
I'll get a stomach-ache.
Then, I'll have to take some **NaHCO$_3$**.
That wouldn't taste
as good as **C$_{12}$H$_{22}$O$_{11}$**."

If you talked like this,
you'd be using chemical symbols
instead of words.

When scientists use symbols like these,
they are describing
just what different chemicals are in things.
The symbols are a short code for the real names
of the chemicals.

H_2O is the chemical symbol for water,
because water is made up of
two parts hydrogen, H, and one part oxygen, O.
$C_{12}H_{22}O_{11}$ is the chemical symbol for sugar,
because sugar is made up of
twelve parts of carbon, C,
twenty-two parts of hydrogen, H,
and eleven parts of oxygen, O.

$NaCl$ is the chemical symbol for table salt,
because table salt is made up of
sodium, Na, and chlorine, Cl.
$NaHCO_3$ is the chemical symbol for baking soda,
because baking soda is made up of
sodium, Na, hydrogen, H, carbon, C,
and three parts of oxygen, O.

Many other things that we see every day
have chemical names that can be shortened
by using the scientist's code.

Here are some other chemical symbols and their meanings.

NH_4OH is ammonium hydroxide,
which is used to clean floors.

H_3BO_3 is boric acid,
which is used to clean sores.

CO_2 is carbon dioxide,
which is used in some fire extinguishers.

$C_3H_5(ONO_2)_3$ is nitroglycerin,
which is used to make dynamite.

$C_9H_8O_4$ is aspirin,
which is used for headaches and colds.

Chemical symbols are especially helpful because
they have the same meanings everywhere in the world.

Money Scribble
$ $ $

Almost everyone recognizes the dollar sign.
But when you stop and think of it,
how did an "S" with two lines through it
ever come to mean dollars?
Why is this symbol used
instead of some other one?

Well, no one knows for sure.
But here are three facts
that may hold the answer.

Fact 1
Once there was a Spanish coin
called a piece of eight.
The eight, or 8, stood for
eight coins, called *reals*.
Each *real* was worth 12½ cents.
12½ times 8 is 100.
So, a piece of eight was worth 100 cents—
the same as an American dollar is worth.

Fact 2
On one side of the piece of eight
were marked the shapes of two pillars.
You can see the pillars
on this picture of a piece of eight.
The pillars stand for the Pillars of Hercules.
The Spanish put the pillars on the piece of eight
in honor of Hercules.

Fact 3
Before Americans had their own money,
they used the Spanish "piece of eight"
and called it "a dollar."

With these three facts, you can use your imagination and say:
    The "S" is a broken 8.
    The "‖" stands for the Pillars of Hercules.
Put them together and you have "$," or the dollar sign—
a "piece of eight" crossed with the Pillars of Hercules.
Nobody really knows where the dollar sign came from.
But this is one explanation—and it might be true.

Howard Pyle painted this picture called **Buried Treasure.**
Pirates often found pieces of eight in buried treasures.

Talking Teepees

When an Indian warrior showed great bravery in battle,
he was a hero to all the members of his tribe.

The warrior painted signs and symbols of his brave deeds
on the outside of his teepee.
Then, the other Indians could always remember
how brave the warrior had been
just by looking at signs on the teepee.
A warrior painted signs and symbols that meant he had

killed an enemy

or scalped an enemy

or captured a gun

or seized a shield

or escaped from an enemy.

Artist Oscar Howe drew picture symbols on a teepee in his painting **Sioux Teacher.**

Some Indians also painted signs and symbols
on their shields and shield covers.
These signs and symbols showed things
that the Indian had seen in his dreams.
The Indians thought that these signs and symbols
would protect them from their enemies.

Lines and Designs for a House

When a house is being built,
the workers can tell
exactly where the different parts
of the house should be,
by looking at special house plans called blueprints.

If you don't know how to read blueprints,
they look like a jumble of lines and designs
that don't make sense.
But the lines and designs
are really marks and symbols,
and they make a lot of sense to the workers.

Some symbols are for the bricklayer.
They tell him what kind of bricks to use.

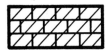 Common brick

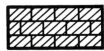 Face brick

Some symbols are for the plumber.
They tell him where to put the pipes and the plumbing fixtures.

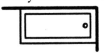 Corner bath

 Kitchen sink

Some symbols are for the carpenter.
They tell him what kind of wood to use.

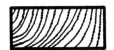 Finish wood

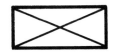 Rough wood

And some symbols are for the electrician.
They tell him what kind of lights and fixtures
he should put in.

 Ceiling outlet

 Wall outlet

Each worker knows what the symbols for his job mean.
And, when he sees these symbols,
he knows what work he's supposed to do.

Star Symbols

"Congratulations! You did very well.
All the answers on your paper are correct."
How could the teacher say all this
without speaking a word?
She stuck a gold star on the paper!
The gold star meant that you did a good job.

But teachers aren't the only ones who use stars.
Generals in many armies wear stars as a sign of their rank.
Famous actors and actresses often have stars
marked on their dressing room doors.
The actors and actresses themselves are even called "stars."
And many sheriffs and policemen wear stars as badges
to show that they are officers of the law.
The Star of Bethlehem and the Star of David
are well-known religious symbols.
And in the United States flag, each star stands for a state.

Printers and writers can use a star called an "asterisk"
to tell you that there is more information
at the bottom of the page or at the end of the chapter.
And where does the word "asterisk" come from?
It comes from the Greek word *aster,* which means *star.*

Now that you know many things that a star can mean,
can you match each picture on the next page with its meaning?

1. good work in school
2. policeman
3. army general
4. famous actor
5. Star of Bethlehem
6. Star of David
7. state
8. asterisk

For answers see pages 312–313.

A

B

C

D

E

F
PATROLMAN
POLICE
1601

G

H

What Does "X" Mean?

X is a letter.
But it's also a number.
And it's also a warning.
And it also can stand for a word.
And it even can stand for a name.
In fact, X can be used in many different ways
to mean many different things.

X is a letter in many different alphabets.
X is the number ten in Roman numerals.
X means an amount that isn't known.
X means multiply.
And X means "this marks a certain spot on the map."

X on a sign beside a highway
can tell you there is a railroad crossing ahead.
X on a sign above a highway
can tell you that a certain driving lane is closed.
X is one of the marks in the game of tick-tack-toe.
X is a sign that means "by"
when we write out measurements,
as in 20' x 15', or "20 feet by 15 feet."

When a voter makes a choice at election time,
he puts an X in a certain square.
The X means "I vote for this man."

And as if these weren't enough things
for X to mean,
you can sign an X to stand for your name,
if you don't know how to write.

Little Marks for Big Words

When you want to figure out
the length of the line that makes a circle,
you have to use the number
3.14159265358979323846. . . .

But if you aren't figuring,
and you just want to write about the number,
it would be a nuisance to write it all out.

So, we use this symbol instead:
 π is a letter of the Greek alphabet, called *pi.*
 π is a short way of writing
3.14159265358979323846. . . .

In math we use many other symbols.

+ means plus or add.

— means minus or subtract.

× means multiply or times.

÷ means divide or separate into equal parts.

= means equals.

$$3 + 3 - 3 \times 3 \div 3 = 3$$

In new math we use different symbols.

{ means the beginning of a set.

} means the end of a set.

⊂ means "is included in."

∪ means "union" and is used almost like a + in addition.

≠ means "does not equal."

∅ means empty set.

$$E = \{1, 2, 3, 4\}, F = \{3, 4\}$$
$$F \subset E, E \cup F = \{1, 2, 3, 4\} \neq \emptyset$$

Mathematics symbols are very useful.
They save time and space.
And they have the same meanings
in all parts of the world.

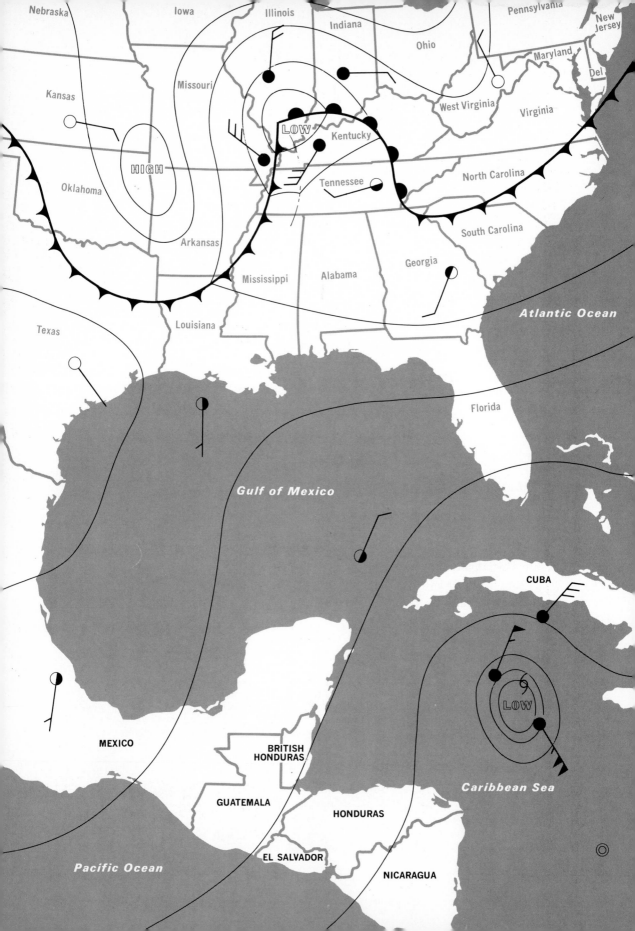

A Look at the Weather

Just by reading a weather map, a weatherman knows
what the weather is like all over the country.
But he doesn't read words or sentences.
He reads circles, flags, and many other scratches and squiggles.

Here are some weather map symbols and their meanings.
Try to find them on the map.

○ means that the sky is clear.
◑ means that the sky is partly cloudy.
● means that the sky is all cloudy.

——— Sometimes a tail
⟍⟍⟍— or a tail with feathers
◣◣— or a tail with feathers and flags
is added to the symbols above
to show how hard the wind is blowing.
For example,
⟍——● means that the wind is blowing
at 9–14 miles an hour.
⟍⟍⟍—● means that the wind is blowing
at 32–37 miles an hour.
◣◣—● means that the wind is blowing
at 119–123 miles an hour.
↶ means a hurricane.
▲▲ means cold front.
◗◗ means warm front.
– – – means heavy thunderstorms.
〜 means that wherever this curved line is drawn,
the air pressure is the same.
Each curved line stands for a different level of air pressure.
The lines are called isobars.

Look at the symbols on the weather map.
What is the weather like in western Tennessee and Kentucky?
In south central Kansas? In North Carolina and South Carolina?
What's happening in the Caribbean Sea?
For answers see pages 312–313.

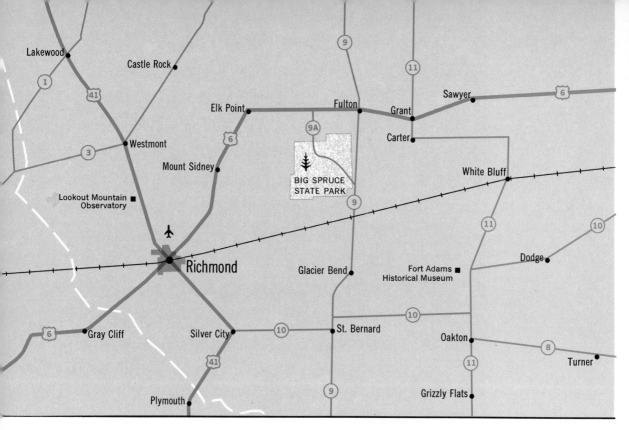

This road map of a make-believe place has marks and symbols
that you find on road maps of real places.

Special Marks on Maps

"How do I get from Richmond to Monroe?
I wonder what interesting places I can see along the way.
I'd better take a look at a road map before I start to drive."

A road map answers a driver's questions
with symbols and marks.
Each symbol or mark has a special meaning.
Somewhere on the map the driver can find
a list of the symbols that are used, with their meanings.
This list is called a legend.
The legend helps him understand the symbols and read the map.

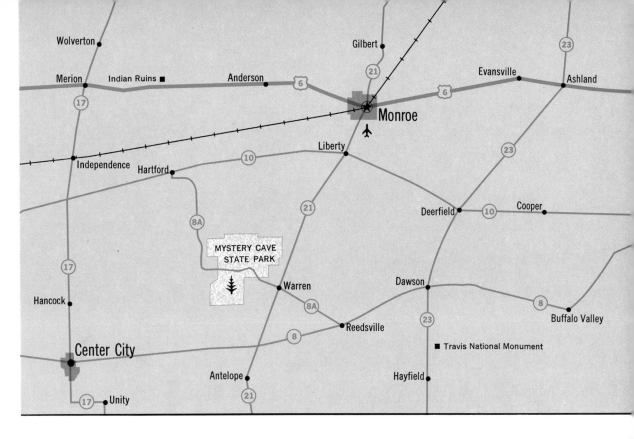

LEGEND

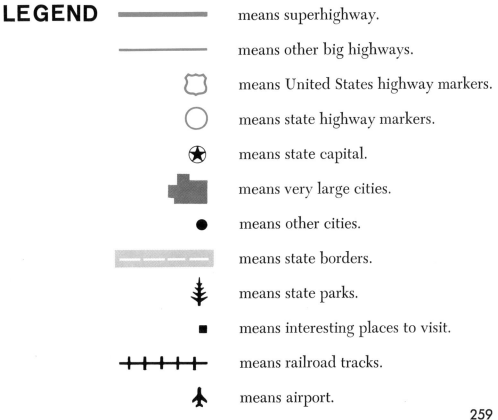

	means superhighway.
	means other big highways.
	means United States highway markers.
	means state highway markers.
	means state capital.
	means very large cities.
•	means other cities.
	means state borders.
	means state parks.
■	means interesting places to visit.
	means railroad tracks.
	means airport.

Signs
for
Hoboes

"Boy! That smells good! It must be fried chicken."
The hungry hobo decided to go up to the house
where the smell was coming from,
and beg for a meal.
As the smell grew stronger, he walked faster.
But, suddenly, he stopped in his tracks.
He saw this sign on the side of the house.
The sign warned him
not to beg for a meal at this house
because "the man inside has a gun."
Hoboes help each other by writing
special picture-messages, or signs,
that tell what to watch out for
or what to do.

The hoboes' special language
has many different signs.
When a hobo draws a picture of a chicken
on the side of a house,
he is telling other hoboes
that the people in the house
will let him use the telephone.

Two overlapping circles mean
"don't give up."

And a sign that looks like a doughnut
means "very good."

Here are some other traditional signs
in the special language of the hobo.

jail   doctor   danger   keep quiet

safe camp   railroad   dog   well guarded house

It Makes Sense

Help What happened to my blue green and yellow marble I
wish I could find it Did I lose it trade it or just misplace it
Maybe Johnny has a marble I can use

What's wrong with this story?
You can hardly tell
where one sentence ends
and the next sentence begins.
Do you know why?
The punctuation marks are missing!
The story doesn't have any question marks
or exclamation points.
It doesn't even have any periods or commas.
Punctuation marks are symbols
that tell you how to read a sentence.
They help a sentence or a paragraph
or a story make sense.

- **.**   A period tells you when a sentence ends.

- **,**   A comma tells you that you should pause
  or take a breath in a long sentence.

- **?**   A question mark tells you that
  the sentence is asking a question.

- **!**   And an exclamation point tells you
  when a word or a sentence says something
  that means a command or a strong and sudden feeling.

When you put punctuation marks in the story above,
it makes sense.
Try to put in the right marks.
For answers see pages 312–313.

TRADEMARKS AND PEOPLE MARKS

Certain special marks and pictures and designs
can tell us something—all without words—
about people, and the things people make.

Marks that help us recognize a thing
or tell us who made it
are called trademarks.

Marks that help us recognize certain people
or tell us something about people
are what you might call people marks.

The next few pages
will show you and tell you about
different kinds of trademarks and people marks.

Soup Cans on the Wall

Once people hung paintings by artists
who painted pictures of heroes and leaders,
people in stories and legends,
places with windmills and rivers.
Artists painted pictures of these things
because people thought these things were important.

Today, some people hang paintings by artists
who paint pictures of such things
as soup cans with trademarks—
things that machines can make by the thousands.

Maybe these artists are trying to prove
that they can do as good a job as a machine can.
Or maybe the artists think that soup cans
and other products with trademarks
are so important to people today
that pictures of these things should be painted.
Maybe the artists are making fun of people
who think such things are important.

What do you think?

100 Campbell Soup Cans, a picture painted by Andy Warhol, ▶
hangs in the dining room of a private home.

A   B   C

Name the Trademark

Just about any picture or design can be used as a trademark—
pictures of people, animals, flowers, trains, planes,
stars, flags, squares, circles, and triangles.
Sometimes words are used as a trademark—
sometimes parts of words, or only a few letters.
The important thing about a trademark—
no matter what it is—
is that people quickly recognize it
and know what product or company it stands for.

Look at the trademarks on these pages.
Can you name the product or company each trademark stands for?
For answers see pages 312–313.

Is It Genuine?

Long ago, when a king passed a law or issued an order,
the paper the law or the order was written on
had to be marked in some way that told everyone,
"This is real. This is genuine. The king really said this!"
The king could just sign his name to the paper,
but then someone else might issue an order
and forge the king's signature on it.

So official papers had to be marked in some special way.
One way would be to drop a blob of hot wax on the paper.
Then the king could press his ring into the wax,
and leave the design of the ring on the wax.
This design was called the king's seal.
Nobody had a seal just like the king's.
So any paper that was marked with a blob of wax
that had the design of the king's seal on it,
had to be genuine, official, and really from the king.

Today, kings and countries,
government officers, cities, states, and provinces,
and even companies have official seals
that are stamped or printed on important papers.

The Great Seal of the United States

The Great Seal of Canada

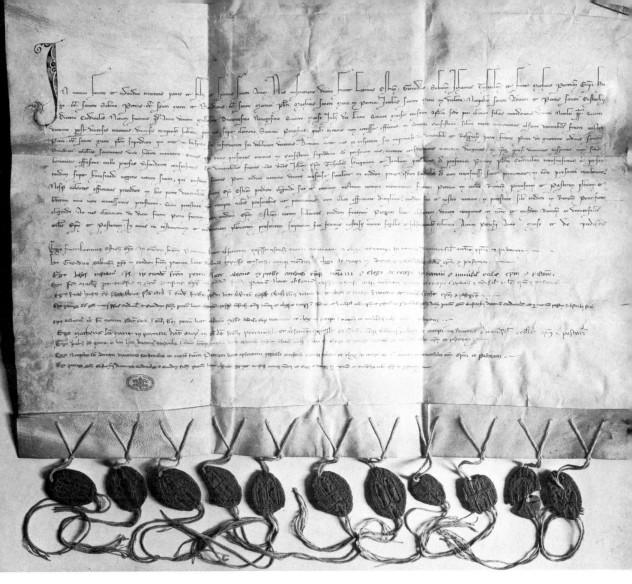

Seals of eleven cardinals of the Roman Catholic Church are attached to this old document. The seals belonged to the cardinals who elected Pope Celestine V long ago.

A governor's seal

A corporation's seal

An architect's seal

Two Knights in Combat by N. C. Wyeth

Coats of Arms

Any knight in armor looked a lot like
any other knight in armor—
a clanking, creaking collection of metal
shaped something like a man.
Then how did one knight know
whether another knight was a friend or an enemy?
He didn't know, unless the other knight
wore a coat over his armor—
a coat with a design that told everyone
who was inside the suit of armor.
We call the design that a knight wore
a coat of arms.

Most people don't wear coats of arms anymore.
But some people still have coats of arms
that show which family they belong to.

Coat of arms
of the Davis family

Coat of arms
of the Kerr family

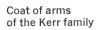

Coat of arms
of Sherman Briggs Reynolds II

Coat of arms
of the Woodward family

Coat of arms
of the Scott family

Royal Coat of Arms
of Great Britain

How
Much
Silver?

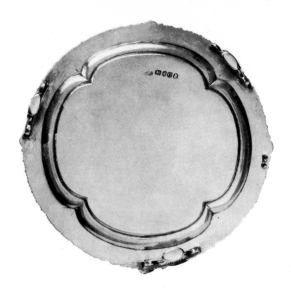

If you saw a silver tray stamped with marks like these,
the marks probably wouldn't mean anything to you.

But they would mean something
to a person who knows a lot about silver.
The first of these marks is called a hallmark.
A hallmark on silver has a special meaning.
Long ago, a king of England ordered
that anything made of silver had to be tested
to make sure it contained the right amount of silver.

The king chose Goldsmiths' Hall in London
as the testing place.
If a silver product passed the test,
the people who tested the silver stamped a mark on it.
This mark was called a hallmark—
from "hall" in Goldsmiths' Hall, and the word "mark."

The king's order started a new custom.
Along with the hallmark, each silversmith
began to stamp his silver with other marks—
a maker's mark to show who made the silver piece
and a date letter to show when it was made.

These four marks are the marks stamped near the top of the silver cup at the left.

The mark, ES, shows the initials of the maker.

This mark shows that the cup was made in London.

This mark shows the high quality of the silver.

This mark shows that the cup was made in 1633.

You can find marks stamped on the backs, fronts, and sides of many silver things. This silver spoon shows the marks stamped on the back.

What Kind of Soldier Are You?

Soldiers in the United States Army
wear pins on their uniforms
that tell you something
about the work they do.

If a soldier wears a pin that looks like this,
it means he's in the infantry.
Infantry soldiers fight with small weapons—especially rifles.

This pin marks a soldier in the artillery.
Artillery soldiers fight with larger guns and rockets.

Soldiers in the Signal Corps wear a pin that looks like this.
These soldiers send and receive messages.
Long ago, the Signal Corps sent most messages by holding
two flags in positions to stand for letters of the alphabet.

Here are some more army pins. Can you figure out why each pin stands for a certain kind of job?

Members of the Ordnance Corps wear this pin. They are in charge of weapons and ammunition.

Military Police wear this pin. They carry pistols, just as ordinary police-men do.

Army engineers wear this pin. They build bridges, dams, forts, and other things.

Members of the Chemical Corps wear this pin. Chemists sometimes use special equipment for experiments.

Members of the Transportation Corps wear this pin. They move men, supplies, and equipment from place to place—sometimes by water.

Members of the Women's Army Corps—or WACs—wear this pin. WACs do many of the jobs that men in the army do.

Members of armored units wear this pin. They sometimes fight the enemy from tanks.

What Kind of Sailor Are You?

You can tell what kind of job
a sailor in the United States Navy has
just by looking at a badge he wears
on the left sleeve of his uniform.
This badge is called a specialty mark.

This is the specialty mark that a radarman wears.
One of the duties of a radarman
is to scan, or watch, radar screens.

A boatswain's mate works with equipment
on the deck of a ship.
At one time, part of a boatswain's mate's job
was dropping the ship's anchor.

A signalman wears this specialty mark.
Part of his job is to use flags to send messages.

Here are some other specialty marks. Can you figure out why each one stands for a certain kind of job?

A gunner's mate wears this specialty mark. He handles the guns and other weapons on a ship.

A boilerman wears this specialty mark. He must be sure that the ship's boiler, or furnace, is working properly, so that the ship will be able to move.

A mineman wears this specialty mark. He takes care of weapons called mines. These are explosives that are dropped into the sea to explode when an enemy ship comes near.

A torpedoman wears this specialty mark.

Guided Missilemen wear this specialty mark. They take care of the navy's guided missiles.

Mechanics wear this specialty mark. They work with tools.

Storekeepers wear this specialty mark. They are in charge of food, clothes, and other supplies.

The insignia of
The Order
of the Garter

The Order of the Garter

Long ago, according to one story,
a king was dancing
with a beautiful lady at a ball
when all of a sudden,
—SNAP!—the lady lost her garter.
It fell to the floor, right in front of everyone.
People began to laugh and whisper to each other.
And of course, the lady was embarrassed.
The king was so angry at the rude people
that he decided to make the garter
the mark of highest honor in his country.

The king was Edward III of England.
He invited important people to join a club.
To belong to the club, they had to wear a special garter.
He called the club, "The Order of the Garter."

Today, hundreds of years later,
it is still one of the greatest honors in England
to belong to the Order of the Garter.

Sir Winston Churchill
was an important member
of The Order of the Garter.

Trademark in the Sky

Riddle: Where can you find a maple leaf flying
thousands of feet high in the sky?

Answer: On an airplane flown by the airline Air Canada.
Air Canada uses a maple leaf in its trademark.

The maple leaf is a popular symbol in Canada.
It is used on many signs and emblems and trademarks.
It is even used on the Canadian flag.

You can see the Air Canada maple leaf
anywhere the airline flies its planes.
The trademark is painted on the sides of the planes.
It is used on the airline's stationery, baggage tags,
flight bags, and in advertisements for the airline.
And if you look closely at an Air Canada uniform,
you'll even see a maple leaf on each button.
The flying maple leaf of Air Canada travels higher, faster,
and farther than any other leaf in the world.
All airlines have trademarks that they use
on many things that they own.

Trademarks That Grow

One kind of trademark grows.
It gets bigger and bigger and bigger
the longer it's been in place.
What kind of a trademark is it?
A cattle brand.
A brand is a cattle owner's trademark.

Cowboys on ranches brand calves
to show who owns them.
As the calves grow, so do their brands.
Here are some brands and how to read them.

Rocking R   When you see a curved line
under a brand, you read it as "rocking."

Swinging Star   When you see a curved line
over a brand, you read it as "swinging."

Lazy 2   When you see a brand on its side,
you read it as "lazy."

Crazy Heart   When you see an upside-down brand,
you read it as "crazy."

Running H   When you see a curvy letter
on a brand, you read it as "running."

Walking E   When you see two "legs" on a brand,
you read it as "walking."

Flying V   When you see "wings" on a brand,
you read it as "flying."

Try to read these brands. For answers see pages 312–313.

SEEING IS BELIEVING?

The title of this book is *Look and Learn*.
Most of the pages in this book show you how,
just by looking at many different things,
you can learn something, know something,
or get some kind of meaning from them.
Almost everything in this book
"says something" without words.
But some things that we see
make us not sure what really is true.
These things are called "optical illusions,"
which is another way of saying
"tricks played on the eyes."

On the next few pages you can see
some of the ways our eyes can play tricks on us.
You can also see how sometimes people make things
that trick our eyes and fool us.

Relativity by Maurits Cornelius Escher

Up the Down Staircases

This picture can make you dizzy
if you look at it long enough.
How?
Try to find out
which way the staircases are going.

The Secret Door

If people want to fool you,
they do something you don't expect them to do,
or they show you something you don't expect to see.

For instance, suppose you saw a doorknob on a wall.
You'd probably think the doorknob was attached to a door.
Maybe you would even grab the knob and try to open the door.
You would be fooled.
You thought the doorknob meant that a door was there.

Sometimes people fool other people
in just the opposite way.
They really have a door in a wall,
but you can't tell that the door's there.
There's no doorknob. You can't see any hinges.
You can't see any cracks that look like they outline a door.
But if you know just where to touch, or grab,
suddenly the secret door will open.

These are kinds of optical illusions.
All they mean is that
you can't always believe what you see.

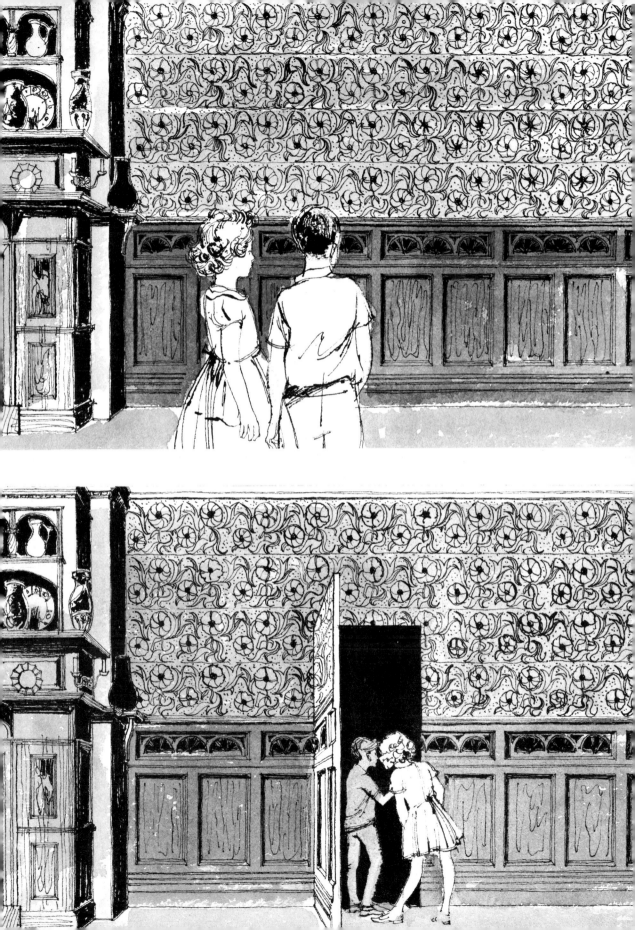

The Magic of Make-Up

This is a picture of a famous clown and actor.
He doesn't look like a clown, though.
That's because he doesn't have any make-up on.
Before you can know he is a clown,
he has to paint his face with the kinds of things
that you see in the picture next to the actor.

When he puts all that make-up on,
he really looks like a clown.
The make-up that clowns and actors put on
makes an optical illusion.
You can't tell for sure
what a person wearing make-up looks like.

Red Skelton as Freddy the Freeloader

How To Hide in Your Clothes

Soldiers fighting in a war have many problems.
One of their problems is to move from place to place
and, at the same time, keep hidden from the enemy.
You can't hide in a hole
at the same time that you move
from one battle position to another.
So you have to use a trick to hide while you move.
Soldiers fighting in countries where the ground is covered with snow
wear white clothes.
The enemy has a hard time
seeing a white-clothed soldier
move in white snow.

Soldiers fighting in jungles wear greenish clothes,
spotted with yellow and brown.
Also, they wear branches and leaves
on top of their helmets.
When the enemy looks around,
all he can see is a green jungle
with small trees and bushes,
spotted with sunlight and dirt—
even though he may be looking right at a soldier.

Coverings that hide anything
by making it look as if it is part of the scenery,
are called "camouflage."
"Camouflage" comes from a French word that means *disguise*.
A camouflage is an optical illusion,
which means things are not always what they seem to be.

A Funny Way of Seeing Things

If you're used to looking at things one way,
and then suddenly you see them another way,
you can be fooled.
The artist who made these pictures
drew them in a way that would fool you
and make you laugh, too . . .
because who ever thought of looking at things
this way?

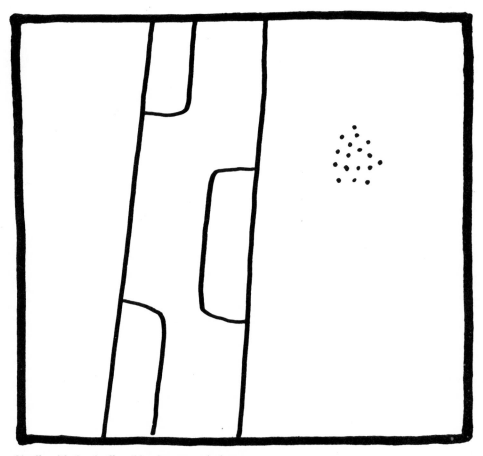

Giraffe with dandruff walking by open window

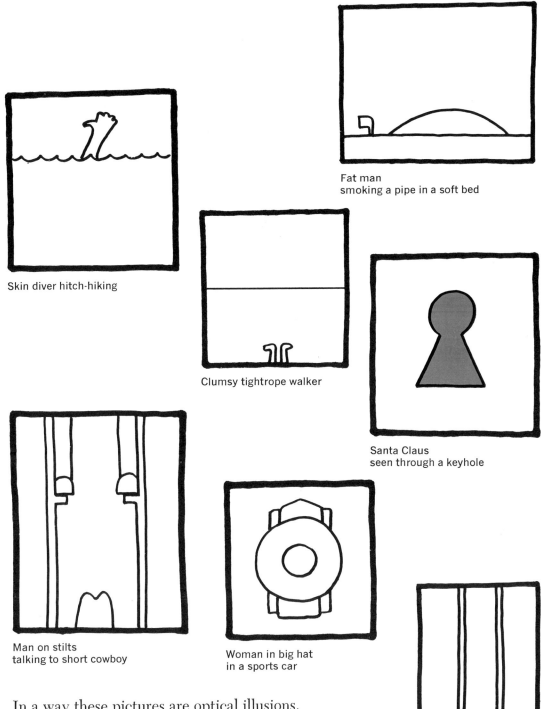

Fat man
smoking a pipe in a soft bed

Skin diver hitch-hiking

Clumsy tightrope walker

Santa Claus
seen through a keyhole

Man on stilts
talking to short cowboy

Woman in big hat
in a sports car

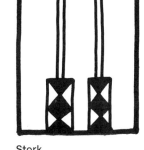

Stork
wearing argyle socks

In a way these pictures are optical illusions.
The artist tricked you into believing
that the pictures don't make much sense—
just by using his imagination
to draw things in a way
that you wouldn't expect to see them.

293

Which Box Holds More?

Packages come in many different sizes.
But some sizes that look different really aren't different.

Mothers have a hard time when they go to grocery stores,
because they know that all the different shapes of packages
may not really be different in size.
It's sometimes hard to tell difference in size by just looking.
And sometimes package makers are so clever
that they can make a package that holds only 100 cookies
look bigger than a package that holds 150 cookies.
Look at the two packages on this page.
Which package looks as if it would hold more?
Both packages hold the same amount.

Different package shapes can make optical illusions.
Things are not always what they seem to be.

"Seeing Into" Pictures

The top picture shows everything flat.
You can't "see into" it.
The picture under it shows
the same scene so that you can see into it.

The artist of the top picture
did not use *perspective*.
"Perspective" comes from
parts of the Latin words
per, meaning *through* or *into*,
and *specere*, meaning *to see*.
When a picture has "perspective,"
it means you can "see into" it.

Really, though, when artists use perspective,
they are using an optical illusion.
The picture is still on a flat surface.
But by making lines go to a point,
called "the vanishing point,"
artists make the picture seem deep,
and make you feel that you can "see into" it.

297

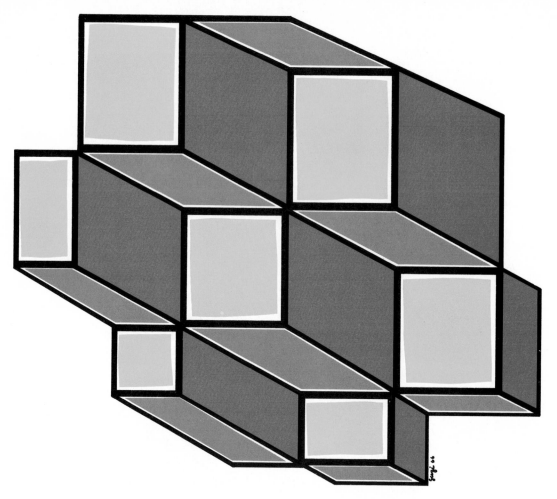

Do you see four boxes or seven boxes?
Either answer is correct.

What Do You See?

Just for fun, some people make up
tricks on the eyes, or "optical illusions,"
to show how our eyes can fool us sometimes.

Here are some of these just-for-fun optical illusions.
See if they work for you,
and then try them on your friends.

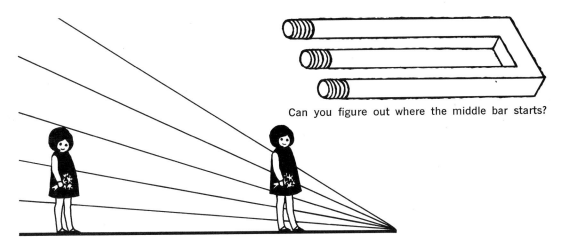

Can you figure out where the middle bar starts?

Which girl is taller? Measure and see.

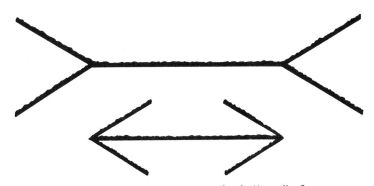

Is the top line as long as the bottom line?

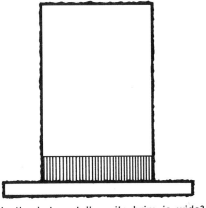

Is the hat as tall as its brim is wide?

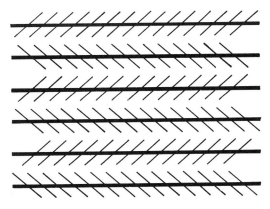

Do the scratches make the long lines slant?

Fooling With Shadows

Some bad men in movies look scary—even without false faces.
But in real life, these men look just like other people.
How can moviemakers make them look so different?
They use shadows!

In real life, light usually hits us
smack in the face or from above.
So the shadows we are used to seeing on faces
are *under* the eyes, noses, and chins.
But what if the light comes from underneath?
Then the shadows won't be where we are used to seeing them.
They'll be above, not below.

Making people look different with shadows
is a kind of optical illusion.
Things that we aren't used to are sometimes scary,
and these strange shadows make a face look scary, too—
even if it isn't really a scary face.

You can see for yourself how the shadows work.
Take a flashlight and sit in front of a mirror in a dark room.
Light the flashlight and hold it under your chin.
See what happens!

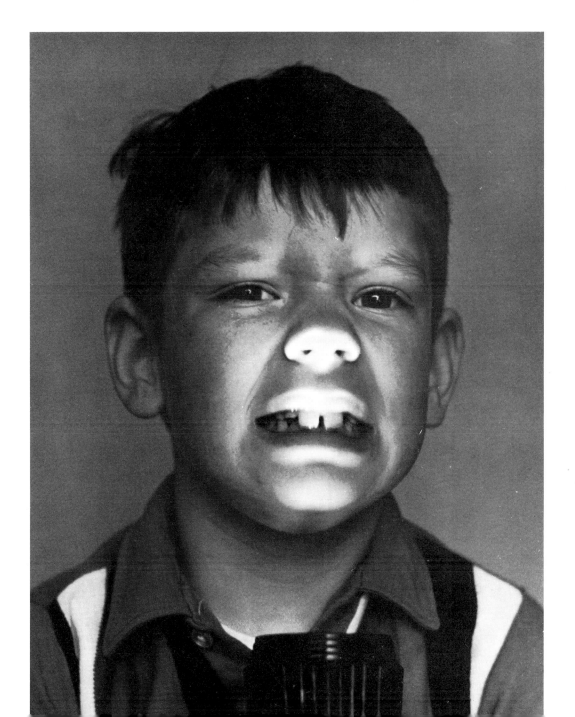

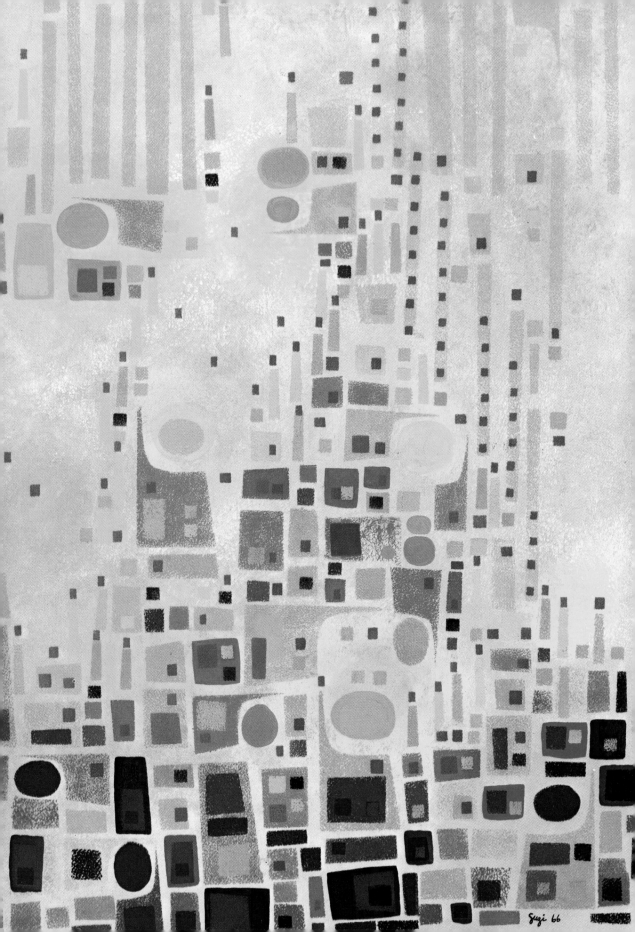

It's Done With Dots

How many colors are in the picture on the opposite page?
  Ten?
  Twenty?
Wrong!

This picture was made with only four different colors—
  blue,
  red,
  yellow,
  and black.

When you look at a small part of this picture
under a magnifying glass,
it looks like the picture below.
You see lots of dots.
If you look carefully,
you see dots of only four different colors.
When your eyes look at the dots,
tiny and close together,
you don't see each separate dot.
You see a blur of many dots.
For example, if half of the dots are red
and half are blue, you see purple.

Usually a printed full-color picture
is a kind of optical illusion.
It makes you see many colors
when really you're seeing only four colors mixed.

Do Moving Pictures Move?

The pictures in movies don't really move.
You just think they do.

When you watch a movie,
you are really watching many, many still pictures.
Each one is slightly different from the one before it.
They flash before your eyes one right after the other—
so fast that you don't see them as still pictures.
Instead, you see changes from picture to picture
that seem to blend.
And those changes seem like movement to you.

How fast do these still pictures move
in front of your eyes?
Twenty-four pictures hit your eyes every single second!
That means that if you watch a movie for one hour,
you have looked at 86,400 pictures!

When pictures seem to move in movies,
it's an optical illusion.
Sometimes you think you see things happening
that are not really happening.

The pictures on these pages give you an idea
of what movie film looks like when it's standing still.

How To Change Color
Without Changing It

Suppose you only have some red paint.
You dip your brush in it,
and paint a spot of red on a piece of yellow paper.
Then you look at it and say to yourself,
"That red is too dark. I want it to look lighter."

But what can you do?
You don't have any other colors
like white or yellow
to mix with the red.
You can't make it thinner.

How can you make the red look lighter
without getting different paint?

Simple! All you do is find a blue piece of paper,
and paint a red spot on it.
Now it looks as if it were a lighter red.
You changed what the color looks like,
but you didn't change the color.
All you did was to put your color next to another color.

Look at the red spots in each of the pictures above.
Believe it or not,
the red spots in each pair of rectangles are the same.
You can prove it by covering the colors around them.

This is a kind of optical illusion.
It means only that things are not always what they seem to be.

Movie Tricks

In some movies or TV shows,
you see whole cities swallowed during earthquakes,
big battleships sunk by torpedoes,
giant animals knocking down buildings
and monsters crushing automobiles in their hands.

Is that what you really see?
No. You are probably seeing
toy cities made of little buildings
like the ones used with model railroads.
You are probably seeing toy battleships
being sunk in a pool.

You are probably seeing close-up pictures
of tiny mechanical animals knocking down toy buildings,
or close-up pictures of a man's hand
crushing a toy automobile.

Moviemakers have to spend lots of money to make movies,
but they could never have enough money
to ruin real cities, or sink real battleships,
or break up real buildings, or crush real cars.
With the help of a camera,
they show optical illusions instead.
Sometimes you think you see things happening
that aren't really happening.

Ships in battles at sea look real in movies. But what you see is an optical illusion
because the ships are really models, such as the one in the picture on the facing page.

People?

If you see tall skinny people
like the ones in the picture,
you might think that you are on another planet.

But the tall skinny people
aren't people at all.
They are shadows of people.
Turn the picture sideways
and you will see.

A photographer is trying to trick your eyes.
He took this picture late in the day
when the sun was in the west.
The sun made tall slim shadows
of the people who were skating.

After he printed the picture,
he turned it sideways
to make the shadows look like people
and the people look like shadows.

ANSWER PAGES

Answers for pages 88 & 89
YOUR FACE
CAN SAY THINGS

A. He's thinking about something funny.

B. He's thinking about something sad.

C. He's thinking about something shocking or scary.

D. He's thinking about something exciting.

E. He's thinking about a disappointment.

F. He's thinking about a surprise.

Answers for pages 96 & 97
TALKING WITH HANDS
AND FINGERS

It's too far to walk!

Answers for pages 118 & 119
PATTERNS ON
YOUR FINGERTIPS

A — D
B — E
C — F

Answers for page 132
POSITION MEANS MEANING

pot — top
tar — rat
nip — pin
was — saw
lean — lane
reap — pear
life — file
owns — snow
lived — devil
north — thorn

Answers for pages 148 & 149
HATS AND SHOES
THAT GO TOGETHER

A — 7   Pirate's hat and boots
B — 6   Cowboy's hat and boots
C — 1   Bullfighter's hat and slippers
D — 3   Jockey's cap and riding boots
E — 9   Robin Hood's hat and pointed shoes
F — 8   Roman soldier's helmet and sandals
G — 2   Dutch girl's hat and wooden shoes
H — 10 Pilgrim's hat and buckle shoes
I — 5   Coolie's hat and wooden sandals
J — 4   Diver's helmet and weighted shoes

Answers for pages 198 & 199
HOT AND
COLD CLOTHES

Winter Clothes

Leather jacket
Fur-trimmed parka
Velvet dress
Wool sweater
Wool coat and muff

Summer Clothes

Cotton shirt and shorts
Cotton dress
Straw hat
Sunsuit
Bathing suit

Answers for pages 230 & 231
SPORTS SETTINGS

Football
Jim Brown
Red Grange
Sam Huff
Otto Graham

Hockey
Eddie Shore
Maurice Richard
Bobby Hull
Gordie Howe

Basketball
Wilt Chamberlain
Bob Cousy

Basketball (cont.)
Oscar Robertson
George Mikan

Baseball
Ted Williams
Ty Cobb
Willie Mays
Mickey Mantle

Boxing
Rocky Marciano
John L. Sullivan
Jack Dempsey
Joe Louis

Answers for page 234
TAKE ANOTHER LOOK

1. The traffic light is tilted sideways.
2. The *ONE WAY* sign is pointing the wrong way: down.
3. The "E" in the *ONE WAY* sign is turned backward.
4. The *CAFETERIA* sign is misspelled.
5. The barber pole is set in front of the cafeteria.
6. The man is rowing his canoe in the street.
7. The bird and the bird's nest are perched upside down.
8. The door on the second floor opens to nowhere.

Answers for pages 250 & 251
STAR SYMBOLS

1 — G	4 — C	7 — E
2 — F	5 — H	8 — B
3 — A	6 — D	

Answers for pages 256 & 257
A LOOK AT THE WEATHER

1. Thunderstorms in western Tennessee and Kentucky. Cloudy sky. Wind, 32 to 37 miles an hour.
2. Clear skies in south central Kansas. Wind, 9 to 14 miles an hour.
3. Hurricane forming in the Caribbean Sea.
4. Cold front moving over North Carolina and South Carolina.

Answers for page 262
IT MAKES SENSE

Help! What happened to my blue, green, and yellow marble? I wish I could find it! Did I lose it, trade it, or just misplace it? Maybe Johnny has a marble I can use.

Answers for pages 266 & 267
NAME THE TRADEMARK

A — General Electric
B — The Bell System
C — Westinghouse
D — Borden's Dairy
E — Quaker Oats
F — Green Giant
G — Radio Corporation of America
H — Gerber Baby Foods
I — Morton Salt
J — Volkswagen
K — Allstate Insurance
L — Sinclair

Answers for page 282
TRADEMARKS THAT GROW

A. Rocking T
B. Swinging B
C. Lazy G
D. Crazy R
E. Walking O
F. Flying W

313

Illustration Acknowledgments

The publishers of CHILDCRAFT gratefully acknowledge the courtesy of the following artists, photographers, publishers, agencies, and corporations for illustrations in this volume. Page numbers refer to two-page spreads. The words "(*left*)," "(*center*)," "(*top*)," "(*bottom*)," and "(*right*)," indicate position on the spread. All illustrations are the exclusive property of the publishers of CHILDCRAFT unless names are marked with an asterisk (*).

COLORS CAN "TALK"

6–7: Gift of the artist, University Art Museum, University of California, Berkeley (*)
8–9: Shelbee Matis
10–11: Herb Kane
12–13: Donald Charles
14–15: (*left*) Jim Jebavy; (*right*) CHILDCRAFT photo by E. F. Hoppe
16–17: (*top*) CHILDCRAFT photos by Don Stebbing; (*bottom*) Joe Rogers
18–19: (*left*) A detail from the mosaic *Emperor Justinian and His Retinue* from San Vitale, Ravenna, Italy — photo from American Archives of World Art, Inc. (*); (*right*) The Lehman Collection, New York (*)
20–21: (*left*) CHILDCRAFT photo; (*right*) Harley Shelton
22–23: CHILDCRAFT photos by E. F. Hoppe and Joseph Erhardt
24–25: World Book Encyclopedia Science Service, Inc.
26–27: CHILDCRAFT photo by E. F. Hoppe
28–29: CHILDCRAFT photos by Lee Balterman
30: Tak Murakami

NOTHING CAN MEAN SOMETHING

32–33: CHILDCRAFT photos by Igor Bakht courtesy Joseph Hirshhorn Collection, New York
34–35: CHILDCRAFT photo by E. F. Hoppe
36–37: (*top*) Betty Fraser; (*bottom*) Dominique Roger, UNESCO (*)
40–41: Michael D. Brown
42–43: George Suyeoka
44–45: Roswell Brown
46–47: (*left*) Suzi Hawes; (*right*) Herbert Lanks, Black Star (*)
50–51: (*left*) Brandt & Associates (*); (*right*) Evans Wollen & Associates, photo from Hedrich-Blessing (*)
52–53: (*left*) Continental Illinois National Bank and Trust Co. (*); (*right*) Shostal (*)
54–55: Joe Rogers
56: CHILDCRAFT photos

SHAPES FROM A TO Z

58–59: (*left*) Anderson, Art Reference Bureau (*); (*right*) Alinari, Art Reference Bureau (*)
60–61: CHILDCRAFT staff art
62–63: CHILDCRAFT staff art
64–65: (*top*) CHILDCRAFT photo; (*bottom*) Richard Loehle
66–67: THE WORLD BOOK ENCYCLOPEDIA
68–69: Design by Suzi Hawes, photography by E. F. Hoppe
70–71: Robert Borja
72–73: Carl Yates
74–75: (*top*) CHILDCRAFT photo; (*center*) Central Press from Pictorial Parade (*); (*bottom, left to right*) The Inaugural Committee, Washington, D.C. (*), The White House, Washington, D.C. (*)

76–77: *De Casibus Virorum Illustrium* by Boccaccio, courtesy Francis Kettaneh (*)

HANDS AND FACES

82–83: The Louvre, Paris — photo from Art Reference Bureau (*)
84–85: John Everds
86–87: CHILDCRAFT photo by Lee Balterman; art by Stan Fleming
88–89: art by Helen Prickett; CHILDCRAFT photos by E. F. Hoppe
90–91: (*top*) CHILDCRAFT photo by E. F. Hoppe; (*bottom*) Helen Prickett
92–93: (*left*) Sidney Rafilson; (*right*) Wide World (*)
94–95: (*left*) Rolf Schaeffer (*); (*right*) Stefan Odry (*)
96–97: Suzi Hawes
98–99: (*left*) Suzi Hawes; (*right*) Hank Kranzler, Stanford Repertory Theater (*)
100–101: Bill Carr
102–103: Betty Fraser
104–105: John Everds
106–107: (*top, left to right*) Maurithaus Museum, The Hague, Netherlands (*), National Gallery of Art, Washington, D.C., Widener Collection (*); (*bottom*) © The Frick Collection, New York (*)
108: CHILDCRAFT staff art

THINGS THAT GO TOGETHER

110–111: The Museum of Modern Art, New York, gift of Samuel A. Berger (*)
112–113: (*left*) Jerry Skolnick; (*right*) Helen Prickett
114–115: (*top*) Jerry Cooke, Photo Researchers; (*bottom*) United Press Int.
116–117: (*left*) CHILDCRAFT photo by Derek Gilby; (*right*) Aerofilms (*)
118–119: CHILDCRAFT staff art
120–121: Ralph Creasman
122–123: Joyce John
124–125: George Suyeoka
126–127: (*left*) National Gallery of Art, Washington, D.C., Andrew Mellon Collection (*); (*right*) Glasgow Art Gallery, Glasgow, Scotland, The Burrell Collection (*)
128–129: (*left*) The National Gallery, London — photo from Art Reference Bureau (*); (*right*) Fernand Hazan, éditeur, Paris (*)
130–131: (*left*) Publix Pictorial (*); (*right*) National Gallery of Art, Washington, D.C., Widener Collection (*); art by Lowell Stumpf
132: Jerry Skolnick

CLOTHES AND TRIMMINGS

134–135: (*left*) The Louvre, Paris — photo from Art Reference Bureau (*); (*right*) The National Gallery, London — photo from Art Reference Bureau (*)
136–137: (*left, left to right*) Mira, courtesy Hurok Attractions, Inc. (*), Alfred Zulliger, Shostal (*); (*right, top to bottom*) H. Armstrong Roberts (*), Werner Stoy, Camera Hawaii (*)
138–139: (*top*) CHILDCRAFT photos by E. F. Hoppe, tartans courtesy of Jofa Inc.; (*bottom*) British Holidays Assoc. (*)
140–141: art by Roy Andersen; photo from The John Woodman Higgins Armory, Worcester, Mass. (*)
142–143: Courtesy *Bride's* Magazine © CPN Inc. (*)
144–145: CHILDCRAFT photos by E. F. Hoppe
146–147: art by Herb Kane; CHILDCRAFT photo
148–149: Betty Ashley
150–151: (*left, top to bottom*) Mile L. Garbison, Shostal (*), D. Forbert, Publix (*); (*right, top to bottom*) Ronny Jacques, Photo Researchers (*), Maynard Williams, Shostal (*), Marc Riboud, Magnum (*)

WHAT MODELS STAND FOR

MATERIALS CAN "TALK"

THE PROPER PLACE

SPECIAL MARKS

TRADEMARKS AND PEOPLE MARKS

SEEING IS BELIEVING?

Index to
Volume 11

This index is designed so that you can easily locate any of the people and pictures, colors and clothes, shapes and materials, or marks and symbols described in this book.

A general index to CHILDCRAFT appears in Volume 15.

318